# *Poor Richard*

## A COMEDY IN THREE ACTS

*By Jean Kerr*

SAMUEL FRENCH, INC.

25 WEST 45TH STREET  NEW YORK 10036

7623 SUNSET BOULEVARD  HOLLYWOOD 90046

*LONDON*  *TORONTO*

POOR RICHARD, by Jean Kerr, directed by Peter Wood, with setting by Oliver Smith, lighting by Peggy Clark, costumes by Theoni V. Aldredge, was presented by Stevens Productions Inc., in association with Lyn Austin and Victor Samrock, at the Helen Hayes Theatre, N.Y.C., on Dec. 2, 1964, with the following cast:

### (*In Order of Appearance*)

SYDNEY CARROLL ............*Gene Hackman*

CATHERINE SHAW ............*Joanna Pettet*

RICHARD FORD ................*Alan Bates*

JOHN McFARLAND ........*Colgate Salsbury*

VIRGINIA BAKER ............*Joan Alexander*

## SYNOPSIS, OF SCENES

### ACT I

Nearly one o'clock in the afternoon. Early April. A bright, sunny day.

### ACT II

Eleven o'clock in the morning, the next day. It has snowed lightly.

### ACT III

After twilight the same day.

# DESCRIPTION OF CHARACTERS

RICHARD FORD: A British poet in his thirties, temporarily in New York. Physically, he might just as easily be taken for a gardener or a truck-driver.

CATHERINE SHAW: An American girl in her early twenties, newly a secretary.

SYDNEY BOLTON: Editor for a large publishing firm in New York. He is only a few years older than Richard, but is the kind of man who always seems ten years older than he is.

GINNY BAKER: Angela's sister. A straightforward girl in her early thirties, impeccably dressed.

JOHN McFARLAND: A writer on Time magazine in his late twenties, easy and intelligent.

## THE SETTING

An apartment in Greenwich Village. We never meet the owner of the apartment, but he is probably a writer.

It is slightly below ground level, so that when double glass doors are opened in the back wall, we see several steps leading up to a narrow terrace, with young, spindly trees beyond.

D. R. are sliding doors which disclose a kitchen with sink, stove, refrigerator, etc. U. L. is a door to the bathroom. A circular stairway leads to a landing from which one enters the bedroom. D. L. is a window out of which we see part of a brick wall and the house next door. The U. S. wall and L. wall are red brick. The R. wall is driftwood panel. The C.S. area is raised. The phone is on jacks—one in the wall L. of the desk and the other in the platform D. S.

There has obviously been a party the night before. A case of empty bottles is under the coffee table. Other bottles and full ashtrays are strewn about, etc.

In general, we are looking toward the rear, not the front, wall of the appartment.

# Poor Richard

## ACT I

*An apartment in the Village. There must have been quite
a party last night, judging from the empty bottles,
glasses, filled ashtrays, etc. The doorbell rings and
rings. Finally,* SYDNEY *lets himself in, with* CATHY.

SYDNEY. Oh Lord, he isn't even out of bed yet. (*Looks
at his watch.*) Quarter of one. I thought even Richard
managed to be vertical by quarter of one. Well, I'll get
him out of there. (*Goes to bedroom door and calls.*) Hey,
Richard! Rich! You've got callers! (*We hear a GROAN,
Off.* SYDNEY *returns to* CATHY.) Don't bother to ask him
how he feels today.

CATHY. (*Mockingly.*) I must say I was terribly
shocked when you told me that Richard Ford drank.
Sydney, honey, it's hardly a well-kept secret.

SYDNEY. (*Fondly.*) Don't you call me Sydney-honey.
I'm still your employer and don't you forget it.

CATHY. You say he just got here yesterday?

SYDNEY. (*Opening drapes and pulling up shades.*)
That's right.

CATHY. How could anybody produce this much of a
mess in twenty-four hours?

SYDNEY. It takes talent and application. (CATHY *has
put away her coat and the enormous, fashionable bag she
carries on a strap over her shoulder and is starting to
clean up the mess.*) And will you tell me why you want
to do this?

CATHY. Because Miss Rodgers is sick and he needs a
secretary.

SYDNEY. (*Taking a sheaf of notes from his briefcase.*)
Yeah, but does he need *my* secretary? There were six
girls I could have sent, but you were so insistent.

CATHY. Not really insistent.

SYDNEY. Oh, *yes* really insistent. I mention most casually that Richard Ford is in town and we're going to have to get somebody to watch over him for a week. Suddenly you are transformed. You are Florence Nightingale, ready to serve. Why?

CATHY. I'm loyal. I'm interested in your writers.

SYDNEY. We have three hundred and forty-one writers and this is the first time I noticed it.

CATHY. I keep things from you.

*(The PHONE rings.)*

SYDNEY. *(Going to phone.)* Well, it starts. *(Picks up receiver.)* Yes? . . . No, I'm sorry, Mr. Ford isn't here . . . Mister who from Time magazine? . . . Mr. Mc-Farland, I'm sorry, I have no idea when he'll be back . . . Very well. *(To* CATHY, *as he hangs up.)* How do they get hold of the number so fast? *(Without pause.)* Cathy, *why* won't you marry me?

CATHY. Because I haven't got a brain in my head.

SYDNEY. You've told me that before. You have to think of another reason.

CATHY. Oh, Sydney, you are sweet.

SYDNEY. The hell with that. I don't want to be sweet. I want to be a bastard and have you love me. Why can't you? Why do—?

*(The PHONE rings again, interrupting him.)*

CATHY. Sydney—the phone.

SYDNEY. Oh, I *hear* the phone. *(Picks it up.)* Hello . . . Mr. Ford isn't here . . . All right, I'll take it down . . . Burbank. . . . California . . . What's the operator again? . . . 27. And the code is 213 . . . Okay, I've got it. *(Hangs up.)*

CATHY. Whose apartment is this?

SYDNEY. It's my brother's. He's in Rome.

CATHY. Why didn't Ford go to a hotel?

SYDNEY. Because he didn't want any publicity. *(PHONE rings again. This time* SYDNEY *is having no nonsense.*) Is this thing on a jack? (*Looks for a wall-jack and finds it.*) Let's pull it out. (*He does.*) He doesn't want to talk to anybody, and it'll just drive you nuts. Cathy, do you realize we're never alone? There are head-waiters, cab-drivers, and I've taken a particular dislike to that elevator man in your building.

CATHY. He's a nice, responsible man. He looks after me.

SYDNEY. But I want to look after you. I feel so old-fashioned about you. I really and truly want to take you on a walking tour of the lake countries. I want to buy you lockets, for God's sake.

CATHY. Sydney honey, we've got to get something done here. (*To kitchen to start coffee.*) I think you should make another effort to rouse the sleeping beauty.

SYDNEY. (*Giving in gracefully, with a small sigh.*) I suppose. (*Going to the bedroom door.*) Hey, there. Hey, Richard. Where's the little boy that looks after the sheep? Come on, sport—up and out of there. (*We hear* RICHARD's *voice saying "Yes, yes, yes."*) There. I've heard definite signs of life. (*Looks at his watch.*) He'd better emerge pretty soon because Allan Brent is waiting for me in the bar across the street.

CATHY. What's with Allan?

SYDNEY. The usual. He's got a block about this new novel. It just won't move. And he thinks maybe he's cracking up because his fingers feel numb all the time. And worse than that, he has a feeling that he screams on the New Haven because people look at him so strangely, and—

CATHY. No, stop! What are you—an editor or a visiting nurse?

SYDNEY. Fifty-fifty.

CATHY. I have no patience with Allan Brent. He's successful, he's rich, and he's famous. What does he want?

SYDNEY. He wants to be happy.

CATHY. Well, he should *be* happy.

SYDNEY. I'll tell him. Cathy, honey, I keep forgetting

how young you are. You don't seem to realize that a poor person who is unhappy is better off than a rich person who is unhappy. Because the poor person has hope, he thinks that money would help. I tell you there is no despair like the despair of the man who has everything.

CATHY. Is that Richard Ford's problem—that he has everything?

SYDNEY. Why do you assume he has a problem? You haven't met him yet.

CATHY. Well, all this drink has to be a sign of something.

SYDNEY. It could be a sign he likes to drink.

CATHY. But he didn't used to, before his wife died, did he?

SYDNEY. No, but what difference does that make?

CATHY. A lot. He's not just an ordinary lush. His wife died and he fell to pieces. There's really something sweet and sad about that—like the nineteenth century. (*Hangs up coat.*)

SYDNEY. You've just given me a clue to something. That is why half the women in America want a signed copy of Girl With Velvet Ribbon. Because it's sweet and sad like the nineteenth century

CATHY. (*Crosses* D.C. *Puts bottles in case. Picks up one woman's shoe—searches for the other.*) Maybe it sells because it happens to be good poetry. Isn't that possible?

SYDNEY. (*Sits chair.*) No, that's not possible. Look, there was fine poetry in "The Apprentice," a fact well known to me and eleven other people. Even the first one has some lovely stuff in it. Did you ever read "The Butter Tower"?

CATHY. Read it?! I used to carry it around with me. I read it on busses. I read it in the bathtub.

> "When first I fell in love with you,
> Like any popinjay,
> I knew a single weather—
> Imperishable May.

"Then simple fields I wandered through
Seemed opulent as parks
And all the weeds were roses
And all the birds were larks."

Remember?

SYDNEY. My dear, I don't remember the second line of "The Star-Spangled Banner." But I see that you are a fan. Then it doesn't surprise you that a handful of poems written to his wife should overnight become—

CATHY. No, it doesn't surprise me at all. Remember what you're always saying. The public will accept anything, even quality. The thing that puzzles me is why he's still lapping it up this way. (*Collects bottles.*)

SYDNEY. See, you're a moralist. You want to know why he's drinking. I'm an editor. I just want to know when.

CATHY. Like what do you mean—when?

SYDNEY. A lot of writers drink. Some drink before they write and some drink after they write. The ones that concern me are the ones that drink instead of writing. Even though a number of people have tried, no one has yet found a way to drink for a living.

CATHY. Oh, Sydney, you're so reasonable. If you were there when Keats was alive, you'd have said, "John, with that cough, you should cut down on the smoking."

SYDNEY. And I'd have been right.

CATHY. I'm not sure you can be reasonable about a talent like Ford's—it happens so seldom. It's an accident of nature—like an earthquake.

SYDNEY. And the best thing to do about an accident of nature is to keep the hell out of the way.

CATHY. (*Rises.*) Meaning?

SYDNEY. (*Rises.*) Oh, meaning nothing. You always duck when I kiss you.

CATHY. (*Crosses to desk.*) I do not. This is working hours.

SYDNEY. Even after working hours. Even when you don't duck, you duck. Cathy, you don't want to notice it but I love you!

CATHY. (*Takes out clipboard.*) Sydney, how can I be efficient if you're going to be fond and foolish? Look, Allan Brent will be gone by the time you get there. And I ought to look over Ford's schedule just in case he ever gets up.

SYDNEY. (*Rises—gives her schedule and pad.*) I know it, I know it. Okay, tell Richard I'll be back immediately. Or almost immediately. And here, this is a list of things he's been asked to do. Some of them he could do—ought to do. Doubtless he won't, but you can bring them to his attention. And this is very important. Tell him to call Ginny Baker.

CATHY. Who's Ginny Baker?

SYDNEY. His sister-in-law. The number is there on the pad. The next thing is that he's here instead of at a hotel . . .

CATHY. Because he doesn't want any publicity, I know.

SYDNEY. Look, you won't be able to keep him from drinking. But it would be helpful—it would be jim-dandy if you could get him to eat something—a lot of something. It'll help to keep him level.

CATHY. And shall I take his 4 P.M. temperature?

SYDNEY. It wouldn't hurt a bit. (*He exits.*)

(*She sits at the desk to open the mail, but there are still several beer cans on the desk and in a moment she sniffs at them, rises, picks them up and drops them into a wastebasket, then goes to terrace windows and opens them. As* CATHY *is returning from the windows,* RICHARD *appears from his bedroom. He is wearing a clean white shirt, though without a tie, and looks very much fresher than we might have supposed. In fact, he is entirely clear-headed, except perhaps about last night. He sees* CATHY. *She stops.*)

RICHARD. Oh, you are a good girl. You remembered.

CATHY. What?

RICHARD. I know I borrowed your lipstick—*some-*

*body's* lipstick—to write the address on a napkin. But I wasn't certain it would be legible. And I'm told that some composer—was it Victor Herbert?—once wrote an entire operetta on a napkin. He must have been very talented, or perhaps it was a bigger napkin. Oh, I am glad you came.

CATHY. You are?

RICHARD. Of course, we'll have to go out for lunch. This place does have that lived-in look, doesn't it? I find myself thinking of the battle of Bosworth Field. Now, *somewhere* I have a jacket—

CATHY. There's your jacket. Now who am I supposed to be?

RICHARD. Why, luv, you are the girl I met in Luchow's last night, the one who lost the earring, who—no, of course you're not. Well, where *would* you like to have lunch? Do you like small out-of-the-way Italian places with melted candles in the Chianti bottles, or are you in the mood for something severe, like the Plaza?

CATHY. Don't you want to know who I am?

RICHARD. Not necessarily. Though I am supposing it will come out.

CATHY. My name is Catherine Shaw and I'm your new temporary secretary.

RICHARD. Oh, oh, oh—'my dear Miss Shaw, this *is* a blow. I must have a drink to absorb this information. If I can *find* one. I must go back to solitary drinking. The real menace of social drinking is that your friends lap up all your liquor. (*He is picking up various bottles, shaking them, finding them empty.*) Ah, here we are! (*Has discovered a vodka bottle with a little something in it.*) Do you know that some people drink vodka because it can't be detected on your breath? I think that's downright dangerous. If a man is going to pass out stone cold, it ought to be clear that he's drunk. You wouldn't want to open your eyes and find a doctor massaging your heart.

CATHY. In case you care, there seems to be a cigarette butt in the bottom of that glass.

RICHARD. I care terribly now that you mention it. Why did you mention it? What did you say your name was?

CATHY. Catherine Shaw.

RICHARD. And you are my new temporary secretary. By the way, what happened to my temporary Miss Rogers, who watched over me last year? Oh, yes, Sydney did call me yesterday. But he was terribly hush-hush and mysterious. I assume her problem is something very delicate and female.

CATHY. I wouldn't say it was all that delicate or female. She broke her ankle. By the way, I didn't know that you were ever in this country before.

RICHARD. Why, I was here for a whole month last year when I made a host of new friends and eventually became known as the scourge of the Biltmore. Also I learned a great deal about the quaint folk customs of the natives. I must say you're a very curious choice for this job.

CATHY. Oh? Why is that?

RICHARD. My secretaries are at least sixty years old— rather chunky, and with blue hair. Margaret Rutherford could play all the parts.

CATHY. (*Crosses* L. *with clipboard to desk.*) Now, shall we get to work? ,

RICHARD. I suppose you have been briefed about me. I mean, you know the worst.

CATHY. That you drink?

RICHARD. That I drink. How chastely you put it. My dear, I'm the last of the great drinkers, internationally known as a tosspot and lush.

CATHY. You're proud of it?

RICHARD. Proud of it? Oh, no, that's too much. Let's say that I'm content with it. Because I know that in my small way I am doing a public service. Now you're not going to believe that.

CATHY. Not yet, anyway.

RICHARD. I am such a comfort to my friends. They have merely to contemplate the spectacle of my disorderly existence and they feel so much better. You know, if you want to be appreciated, really appreciated, the thing to do is to be a bad example.

CATHY. Very well, I shall take that as my thought for day. (*Crosses to desk.*)

RICHARD. Dear me. Everything you say is a period.

CATHY. What should it be?

RICHARD. It should be a question-mark—or at the very least, a comma. It's almost as bad as if you kept saying—"Oh really?"

CATHY. Would you like something to eat? (*Starts for the kitchen.*)

RICHARD. No, but would *you* like something to eat?

CATHY. No, but then : m not the one who—

RICHARD. —who's drinking.

CATHY. That didn't come out very gracefully, did it? (RICHARD *crosses to desk for cigarette.*) Look, I'm not an undercover ageny for A.A. Furthermore, I have no little secret plan to rehabilitate you in five minutes. But there are things to be done. I get paid, you know. Maybe you should give me some kind of a hint. What do people *do* about you?

RICHARD. What do they do? Nothing. They worry and make little clucking sounds. (*Sits desk chair. Imitating them.*) "Poor Richard—and he's so talented. If he'd only straighten himself out. At the rate he's going he won't last till he's forty. It's just a *crime,* such a waste—"

CATHY. Do you say that little speech a lot?

RICHARD. Why?

CATHY. Because it sounded mechanical—like a pre-recording. As though you were so familiar with the words you'd forgotten what they meant. . . . Well?

RICHARD. I think that's really rather perceptive of you. (*Looking directly at her with new interest.*) Who *are* you, Miss Catherine Shaw?

CATHY. (*Sits basket chair.*) Oh, I'm just a girl. I have blond hair, I'm five-feet-two, I—

RICHARD. I didn't ask to see your driver's license. I want to know—are you really this clear-eyed, this serene?

Is there nothing that puzzles you? Are you never perplexed?

CATHY. I'm sure I must be. Everybody is.

RICHARD. Ah, yes—but not you. I see that your mind is all made up, like a roomette on the Pennsylvania. I see I'm not going to get a rise out of you. So we might as well to our chores. (*Noticing that she is snapping her watch-band.*) Angela, my wife, used to pull at her watch-band like that. I warn you. They break.

CATHY. Yes, I've found that out, and I must stop it.

RICHARD. (*Picks up clipboard. At the desk.*) What do we have that's colorful or interesting on this list? By the way, if I'm invited to the White House, get me out of it. I'm told they have scenes from Shakespeare after dinner.

CATHY. (*Crosses to* RICHARD.) The first thing you're supposed to do is call Ginny Baker. I have the number here.

RICHARD. I'm afraid that's the last thing I'm going to do.

CATHY. (*Surprised.*) Oh?

RICHARD. Ginny Baker is my very rich sister-in-law. She was born with a silver foot in her mouth. (*Abruptly terminating this line of thought.*) Next subject?

CATHY. (*Puzzled but going on.*) There are all these copies of "Girl With Velvet Ribbon" that Sydney wants you to sign.

RICHARD. Not until my wrist is better.

CATHY. Well, there is a Mr. Irving Loesser in California who is trying to get in touch with you. (*She has gone to the telephone.*)

RICHARD. I know, I've already had five cables.

CATHY. What does he want?

RICHARD. I haven't the faintest idea.

CATHY. We'll find out. (*Plugging in the telephone jack.*)

RICHARD. What if I told you I wasn't curious?

CATHY. Everybody is curious about long distance calls. You might as well talk to him and put an end to the cables. (*Dials long distance.*) Operator, I want to pick up a call . . . Operator 27 Burbank, California . . . All right. (*She waits.*) Yes, one minute please. (*Hands phone to* RICHARD *and exits kitchen.*)

RICHARD. (*Sits sofa. On phone.*) Richard Ford here . . . Yes, I did. (*Pause.*) That's right, I didn't. (*Pause.*) You're making a movie called what? . . . "The Golden Age of Pericles" . . . Yes, I recall that he was Greek . . . No, I didn't know him personally . . . That's correct, I'm joking . . . I see . . . I see . . . But if you have five writers, what the hell do you want with me? . . . I see . . . I'd have to be there Monday. What's the rush? . . . And why would I want to do this? . . . I agree with you. Forty-five thousand dollars is a perfectly good reason, but I'm afraid I'm not interested . . . Sure, I can let you know tomorrow, but why don't I let you know today? . . . All right, all right . . . 'Bye. (*Hangs up. To* CATHY, *who appears in kitchen doorway with tray and coffeepot and cups.*) He wants me to sleep on it. You see, Mr. Loesser is not only a producer of vision, he is a natural-born phrasemaker. Actually I'd sell my soul for forty-five thousand dollars, but he probably isn't interested in my soul.

CATHY. (*Picks up clipboard.*) Now. The Academy of Arts and Letters want you to be guest of honor at a dinner to be given—

RICHARD. No dinners. I'm on a diet.

CATHY. (L. *of sofa.*) Then there's all these television shows. It appears that you are wanted, needed, on the Tonight show, the Today show. Sydney says to say "no" to all of them. Is that right?

RICHARD. That's right.

CATHY. I must admit that when he told me you never would go on television, I thought it was because you were shy and inarticulate.

RICHARD. Well, I *am,* but I thought it would take you longer to find out.

CATHY. (*Ignoring the remark.*) *And* the Ladies' Home Journal will pay you two thousand dollars for two thousand words on the general subject of—here, let me get this—oh, yes—"What I Learned From Women."

RICHARD. Oh, what rogues they are! It's things like that that convince me our civilization is doomed. Two thousand dollars for that bilge. Do you know Mozart only got five hundred dollars for "Don Giovanni"?

CATHY. (*Syly, matching him.*) That's disgraceful! Who was his agent?

RICHARD. Do you know, I think I'm going to like you, Miss Catherine Shaw.

CATHY. (*Not abashed.*) Well, good. Then you can call me Cathy. Here's something from the Association of American Librarians. They just want a list of the books you are reading currently.

RICHARD. Look, luv, I don't have a reading list any more. I just read the writers that make me laugh— Benchley, Thurber, Faulkner. (*She tries not to smile. RICHARD rises to her.*) If you smiled—a very small smile—I wouldn't take it as approval. (*He goes to window.*) This part of the Village is very little different from my street in London. Gray stone steps, a wilderness of gray stone steps. And those stunted little trees. Even the new April leaves seem dried up. There's something so wistful about those trees. As though they were thinking, "Well, we're a lot better than nothing." But I do miss my hat hospital.

CATHY. Your what?

RICHARD. I don't expect you to believe me, because I am notoriously untrustworthy and I always exaggerate. But I really and truly do live across the street from something called The Hat Hospital.

CATHY. (*Sits chair.*) For hats—ailing hats?

RICHARD. That's what I suppose. I see cars arriving at all hours, and I keep imagining the poignant scene. "Doctor, this is my little blue straw, and I'm so worried. Oh, I blame myself. I knew on Monday when I looked at that feather that something terrible was the matter. It isn't too late, is it, Doctor?" "Well, I must tell you, in all frankness, Madam, I don't like the look

of that brim. If we had got it forty-eight hours ago—or
even if it had been felt. We're getting dramatic results
with felt." "And doctor—when are the visiting hours?
When can I see it?" (CATHY *is now laughing, feeling at
home with him finally, and* RICHARD *notices*.) Ah, now—
there you are. That was such a lovely smile. Now, are
you going to kiss me?

CATHY. No, but I'm enjoying your performance. I'll
bet you sing, too.

RICHARD. (*After a pause.*) The polite thing would
have been to slap my face.

CATHY. When you're being so winning, and climbing
into my heart this way?

RICHARD. Oh, you *are* patience on a monument, aren't
you? The air must be very thin up there. Do you find
the breathing difficult?

CATHY. Not really. (*Debates with herself for a second,
then turns toward him.*) Look, I think I'd better be
honest with you. I'm not the least bit offended, but in
the circumstances I really don't think you should be
making passes at me.

RICHARD. Why not?

CATHY. (*Quietly, going about her work.*) Because
you're going to marry me.

(*She has said this so matter-of-factly that* RICHARD
*almost doesn't catch it. Then he does.*)

RICHARD. (*Approaching her, gaping.*) That's why I
hate to fly the Atlantic. For days afterward I don't hear
things correctly.

CATHY. Oh, you heard me correctly. Now this pile of
letters is mostly invitations to lecture. I presume the
answer is no.

RICHARD. (*Sits stool.*) Have you recently come out of
an institution?

CATHY. I came out of the Columbia School of Jour-
nalism last June, but I'm sure that isn't what you meant.

RICHARD. I mean are you mad? Do you propose to every man you meet?

CATHY. Hardly.

RICHARD. Well, I can be forgiven for asking.

CATHY. What you don't understand is that I've thought about this for a long time—for years. And I think the mistake most people make about marriage is that they let it *happen* instead of doing something about it. See, I think you should have a *reason* for marrying somebody.

RICHARD. Oh, I'm *with* you on that.

CATHY. But I mean a real reason. Because you get chills running up and down your spine is no reason.

RICHARD. No?

CATHY. That lasts about one year. In a relationship that's going to have any permanence, *everything* else is more important. What you're looking for is an equation with the least number of variables. Now, I admire your work, but even that isn't the point. The point is that your habit of thought interests me, pleases me. And I expect it always will. I mean, it won't thin out on me. Now you're going to say, "Okay, that's your reason, what's my reason?"

RICHARD. I'm not going to say one damn thing.

CATHY. Okay. Good, but listen to me. With your wife, you *had* romantic love. And you're probably not looking for it again. In any case, the chances are you wouldn't find it. But you ought to have somebody. Now you may not find me terribly interesting, but I am clear-headed. I don't want to antagonize you, but it must be obvious, even to you, that you could use somebody clear-headed.

RICHARD. By God, you *mean* it.

CATHY. Did you think I was joking? Marriage is a serious matter—especially for me. I don't believe in divorce, which means I plan to have only one husband.

RICHARD. Me.

CATHY. That's right.

RICHARD. What if I told you I had other plans?

CATHY. You won't.

RICHARD. *How* did you get to be so positive? You sound as though you'd just received a telegram from God. I keep thinking I should ask, "And how are the apostles?"

CATHY. Oh, I am positive, and actually it's worse than you know. Other people are positive about big issues, like nuclear testing and euthanasia. I'm positive about Jerry Lewis and paper napkins.

RICHARD. (*Rises.*) Oh, where is my nice, dreary Miss Rogers?

CATHY. She broke her ankle. I told you.

RICHARD. This offer of yours. Is it for a limited time only? When does it expire?

CATHY. Why do you keep wanting to *talk* about it?

RICHARD. (*Explosively.*) I'm *interested!*

CATHY. Well, I'm not, and you make me sorry I told you. (*Marking the letter.*) Now. Next, do you want to have lunch with a Mr. Edwards from NBC? He hopes to interest you in writing a verse play that could be done next Easter. It would be a ninety minute spectacular.

RICHARD. (*Crosses R. end of sofa.*) It sure as hell would. No, of course not. No.

CATHY. Oh, dear, now you're cross and irritable and I feel responsible.

RICHARD. I am not cross. I am *not*—

CATHY. Maybe you ought to have a drink.

RICHARD. If your plan is to drive me crazy, you are nicely on the way. You're not supposed to ask me to have a drink. You're supposed to lock up the bottles and carry on about the glories of Coca-Cola and black coffee!

CATHY. (*Crosses to desk.*) Of course, if you *want* some coffee—

RICHARD. I have your permission. Look, dear Miss Manic-Depressive. I want to know something. Granted your convictions, how is it that I haven't heard from you before?

CATHY. Oh, you have.

RICHARD. (*Startled.*) When?

CATHY. I wrote to you when I was fifteen years old.

RICHARD. Well, I never got it.

CATHY. But you did.

RICHARD. What makes you think so?

CATHY. Because you answered.

RICHARD. (*Skeptically.*) Oh, I did? Really? And what did I have to say?

CATHY. (*Going to her purse and getting out a post-card.*) I'll show you. You may not be able to read it. It's kind of blurred. That's because I let it fall in the bathtub once. (*She hands it to him.*)

RICHARD. (*Reading.*) "Dear Miss Shaw, thank you for your letter. I'm glad you love the book. I'm glad you love me. Please notify me when you come of age. With all good wishes. P.S. I—" (*He frowns over the P.S., then something hits him.*) Oh. Oh, yes, yes, yes, I think I do remember. Aren't you the girl who said you were going to pray for me?

CATHY. That's right.

RICHARD. (*After staring at her for a moment.*) Do you still pray for me?

CATHY. Yes.

RICHARD. (*With a sigh, and dismissing it all.*) Well, I suppose it doesn't do any harm.

CATHY. Don't you believe in anything?

RICHARD. I used to believe in words. I used to believe in poetry. Get me to tell you sometime how I fell out of love with the English language.

CATHY. (*Unaffectedly.*) And you don't believe in a hereafter?

RICHARD. I don't believe in a *here*. You do, I gather.

CATHY. Certainly.

RICHARD. And you believe in an actual heaven and an actual hell?

CATHY. Yes.

RICHARD. With little devils shoveling on red hot coals—?

CATHY. (*Now impatient herself.*) Why do people go on about little devils and red hot coals? We're not told

there will be a fire necessarily. It may just be a sense
of *loss.*

RICHARD. You mean it's not the heat, it's the humidity.

CATHY. You haven't even thought about this. You
are merely taking an attitude. That's something else
we'll have to change. (*Sits desk chair.*)

RICHARD. (*Blowing, really mad now.*) *Listen* to her!
You have a mind like an electric Blendor. You think you
can go *bzzzzz* and all the litttle lumps will be gone!
You come on down from Olympus, honey, and take a
look at the natives. They are not simple. Nothing is
simple, nobody is simple. The girl who wraps packages
in the basement of Bloomingdale's is complicated beyond
anything you could imagine! The elevator boy who—

CATHY. *Now* would you like a drink?

RICHARD. I do not want a drink. What I want is for
you to go home or back to the office or into the woodwork
or wherever you came from and leave me alone with my
memories and my sanity! (*Starts for the bathroom.*)

(SYDNEY *enters.*)

SYDNEY. Greetings.

RICHARD. (*Hurrying to him and embracing him
heartily.*) If it isn't Friar Lawrence! Dear ghostly father, I've missed you! And how the hell are you?

(CATHY *has quickly and quietly reverted to the desk
and her work.*)

SYDNEY. I'm marvelous. I've lost ten pounds and I
have two best-sellers and what else is there?

RICHARD. Nothing.

SYDNEY. How are you and Miss Shaw getting along?

(*There is a moment's silence, with a slight bristle to it,
as* RICHARD *glances at Cathy, and as* CATHY'S *eyes
look up from her work, without turning toward
them. Brief as this is,* SYDNEY *notices it.*)

CATHY. (*Glossing over the moment efficiently, rising.*) I think Mr. Ford is still exhausted from the plane trip. I think I'd better go out and get him a sandwich.

(CATHY *goes out the front door.* SYDNEY *is aware of something in the air.* RICHARD *looks after Cathy for a moment, then makes a controlled gesture in her direction.*)

RICHARD. Tell me about that.

SYDNEY. Miss Shaw? Well, she's my secretary. She's —apparenty a big fan of yours.

RICHARD. Yes, in her shy way she made that very clear.

SYDNEY. (*With a shade of meaning, a wistful warning.*) Well, she's very young.

RICHARD. But not seven?

SYDNEY. No, not seven. (RICHARD *goes into the bathroom. Brightly, changing the subject. He doesn't want to think about what might possibly go on between them.*) Okay, I want to know. Why didn't you answer my letters?

RICHARD. Which letter?

SYDNEY. Any of them. Let's start with the first one. Three months ago I wrote and told you "Girl With Velvet Ribbon" was going into a third printing. I expected howls of joy. Hell, I thought you might send me some pressed violets, or even a small white Cadillac. Instead of which, silence—total silence.

RICHARD. (*He has not forgotten the demon outside.*) Forgive me, Sydney. I'm afraid I'm a rotten pen-pal.

SYDNEY. I'll forgive you if you tell me you've been putting all your time on the new book.

RICHARD. (*Crosses* R. *and sits sofa.*) What new book? I haven't written a word in eighteen months.

SYDNEY. Why not?

RICHARD. You know what Robert Benchley used to say when people asked him why he'd stopped writing books. He said he'd shot his bolt composing humorous telegrams to friends who were going on vacation.

SYDNEY. That's what Benchley used to say. What do you say?

RICHARD. Nothing. Except to remind you of that old Spanish proverb, "How beautiful it is to do nothing—and rest afterwards."

SYDNEY. (*Sits sofa. Keeping at it, and genuinely concerned.*) It's curious that people only tell you Spanish proverbs when they don't want to tell you the truth. What is the truth? I keep reading ever more colorful stories about your ever more colorful binges. What's with you, Rich?

RICHARD. (*Deflecting the serious tone.*) I'm glad you asked me that, Sydney. Because I have a problem. This back tooth of mine has been acting up. Now the dentist says he could file it down and put a crown on it. On the other hand—

SYDNEY. Okay, you're not going to tell me. You'll be happy to know we hit 80,000 copies of "Girl" last week. That's a lot of copies.

RICHARD. (*Crosses to kitchen.*) Yes, I figure it must be poisoning the very air we breathe. By the way, who got the bright idea of calling it "Girl With Velvet Ribbon"?

SYDNEY. I guess I did. We needed a title so I pulled a line out of the first poem. "Though tick-tock time devours—" (RICHARD *and* SYDNEY *together.*) "all that is born and grieves, the Girl With the Velvet Ribbon . . ."

RICHARD. (*Returning with a drink.*) I know the poem. The title still sounds as if it were written by an elderly lady with three names. Look, Friar Lawrence—out with it. Why did you bring me over here?

SYDNEY. (*Sensing a suspicion in* RICHARD *and answering a bit too quickly.*) Wait a minute. You said on that postcard that you were getting lonesome for Whalen's Drug Store.

RICHARD. Well, it's perfectly true that I have a passion for Whalen's—where else can you buy a copy of "God's

Little Acre" and a tin of Ex-Lax while you're waiting
for a tuna salad sandwich? I certainly wasn't planning
to cross the ocean about it until I got your cable "Important that you be in New York Sunday, April seven-
teenth." Now that's the day after tomorrow. What's
happening?

SYDNEY. (*Cornered and facing it.*) Okay, I'll tell you.
(*Speaking carefully and directly to Richard.*) You
know, of course, that Angela's father and mother gave
a lot of money to the New York Hospital.

RICHARD. I heard something about it.

SYDNEY. What they did, actually, was build a wing
onto the hospital itself. It will be called the Angela Ford
Memorial Wing.

RICHARD. I see.

SYDNEY. I gather it's quite something. Anyway, the
official dedication and opening will be on Sunday. The
Mayor will make a speech and so forth, and I thought
you ought to be there.

RICHARD. (*Letting fly.*) For the publicity? To get my
picture in the paper? "Weaving figure at the left is the
bereaved husband!" By God, the boys in promotion will
do anything to sell four copies, won't they?

SYDNEY. No, not for the publicity. I can give you the
conventional reasons. This is a memorial to your wife,
and it's your place to be there. Furthermore, it would
please Mr. and Mrs. Howard. What I'm debating with
myself is whether or not I should take the risk of giving
you the real reason.

RICHARD. Please do.

SYDNEY. (*Plainly.*) I think it may be necessary for
you to do this.

RICHARD. Necessary? I don't understand.

SYDNEY. I think soon you will have to believe that
Angela is dead.

RICHARD. (*Frowns, stares at him.*) I believe it.

SYDNEY. There are different kinds of belief. I believe
that today is Friday. And I believe that one day I will
die—but I don't believe them in the same way.

RICHARD. Oh, for God's sake, Sydney, *say* what you're trying to say!

SYDNEY. I'm saying that rituals are important. They mark the event. They put a circle around it so you can feel it and see it. For instance, you'd have been much better off psychologically if you'd gone to Angela's funeral.

RICHARD. You make it sound as though I simply couldn't fit it into my busy schedule. I was in the hospital with pneumonia.

SYDNEY. That doesn't change anything. The point is you weren't there. For you the event has never taken place. For that reason alone, you ought to be at the ceremony at the hospital.

RICHARD. You think it'll be practically as good as a funeral.

SYDNEY. (*Sharply.*) I'll tell you what I think. I think grief is a decent human emotion, but it is not a career. (RICHARD *wheels on him; this barb has struck home.*) Richard, I'm sorry for that.

RICHARD. (*With a great restraining sigh.*) It's all right.

SYDNEY. No, it's not all right. I've offended you—and offended you without convincing you.

RICHARD. (*Trying to hold himself in check, but with difficulty.*) Sydney, listen to me. You are not going to offend me, now or ever, because I know your affection for me. But will you for God's sake leave my psyche the hell alone! I keep feeling that you're trying to draw me out like a friendly psychiatrist—teasing me up the path of self-knowledge. I don't want to know any more about myself. The subject bores me. I'm afraid my small romance with myself is over. And I see what you're thinking. You're thinking—ah! that's very significant, we're getting warmer. (*Running on.*) Look, the way I feel or the way I behave is not really that important. Let's save our concern for real issues, like the spread of Communism in South America, or teen-age dating. Did you know that in this country there are thousands of ten-year-old Cub Scouts who are going steady? By the time they're fourteen, they'll be already divorced! (SYDNEY *says nothing*.) And as far as that goes, who the hell do you know that is so bloody well-adjusted?

SYDNEY. Nobody. But most of the people I know manage to operate.

RICHARD. Meaning?

SYDNEY. If they're writers, they write. If they're plumbers, they plumb.

RICHARD. Oh, is that what bothers you? That I don't plant 'taters and I don't plant cotton! Well, be cheered. As of Monday, I join the ranks of the employed.

SYDNEY. Where?

RICHARD. Hollywood.

SYDNEY. I don't believe it.

RICHARD. (*Crosses to desk for cable.*) No, I'm going to work on a movie about Pericles. Surely you remember that lovable old character, Pericles!

SYDNEY. When did you decide this?

RICHARD. Recently. But I'll be flying out of here tomorrow, so I won't be here for the ceremony at the hospital.

SYDNEY. (*Crosses L. to* RICHARD.) You're going to do a screen play? (*He is unbelieving.*)

RICHARD. (*Shows the cable.*) No, I just take the existing dialogue and give it some class.

SYDNEY. (*Wryly.*) And how do you do that?

RICHARD. I imagine you add words like "yon." "Do you think yon peasant can be trusted?" No, no. "Is yon peasant to be trusted, *think* you?"

SYDNEY. (*Giving back the cable.*) Richard, this is disgusting. Surely you have learned by this time that you cannot work for a medium you patronize.

RICHARD. I thought you were the one who loved movies.

SYDNEY. You're damn right. I grew up on them. I was twenty-five years old before I saw a bad movie. But we're talking about you, and you despise them.

RICHARD. Are you mad? You see before you a man

who saw Shirley Temple in "Bright Eyes" nine times!
Shall we ever forget— (*Goes right into song, with a
faint imitation of Shirley Temple's cuddly tones.*)
    "On the good ship Lollipop,
      It's a sweet trip to the candy shop. . . ."

(*In the middle of this,* CATHY *returns with a bag of
    sandwiches. She stares at what he is doing.*)

CATHY. But you *should* go on the Ed Sullivan show!
RICHARD. (*Going right to her, using deep, earnest
tones, mockingly.*) You really think so? You're not just
trying to make me feel good? I mean, you're *serious?*
(*Turning to* SYDNEY.) Sydney—tell me—where did you
find Miss Know-it-all here?
SYDNEY. (*Hearing the "Know-it-all" and still trying
to gauge what has gone on between them.*) And what
does that mean? Have I missed something?
CATHY. (*Cutting in.*) He didn't find me. I found him.
(*Crosses* L. *and sits desk.*)

(RICHARD *cocks his head at* SYDNEY, *as if for con-
    fimation.*)

SYDNEY. (*Crosses to* RICHARD.) That's true. Miss
Shaw wrote me a letter asking for an interview. Then
one afternoon she came in to see me and announced that
she'd been thinking the matter over and wanted to be
my secretary.

(RICHARD *looks at Cathy.* CATHY *simply and demurely
    pours coffee.*)

RICHARD. I see. And you went right along with this
idea?
SYDNEY. No, I did not. I told her I already had a
secretary—a jewel of a secretary who was in fact the
only comfort of my declining years.
RICHARD. Oh, sure—Clarkey. And what happened to
her?

SYDNEY. (*Enjoying his story.*) Let me tell you. I finally got it through to this one that I am entirely satisfied with my present help. So she said, "Fine, but I'm going to leave you my telephone number in case anything happens to her."

CATHY. (*Placidly.*) Sydney, this can't be interesting to Mr. Ford.

RICHARD. No, no. It holds—it has suspense—

SYDNEY. I said, "Nothing will happen to Clarkey, she's in the very bloom of health."

RICHARD. She poisoned her.

SYDNEY. (*Sits R. end of sofa.*) No, three weeks later in comes Clarkey—my forty-three-year-old Clarkey, all smiles and girlish confusion. After seventeen years of marriage she's finally pregnant.

RICHARD. Well! Good for Clarkey!

(*But his mind is on* CATHY, *whose own mind is unruffled. We are aware of the contest of will between them throughout.*)

SYDNEY. That was *her* attitude. My attitude was that I'd like to shoot her husband, especially since she felt she had to quit immediately because she wanted to be extra-careful on account of her age and so on and so on.

RICHARD. (*Pursuing the inevitable.*) And immediately you thought of Miss Shaw.

SYDNEY. No, I didn't. I interviewed about seven idiots. The last one informed me she'd like to keep her nails, so she'd need an electric typewriter. *That's* when I thought of Miss Shaw.

RICHARD. (*With absolute concentration.*) But the point remains—Miss Shaw *announced* she was going to be your secretary, and she *did* become your secretary.

SYDNEY. (*Thinks, grins, and nods.*) That's about the size of it.

RICHARD. Excuse me. I have to make a phone call. (*With great decisiveness,* RICHARD *takes an address book out of his pocket on which some names seem to be*

*written, decides on one, and reaches for the phone, only
to get no dial tone.*) The lines have been cut.

(*With a patient glance,* CATHY *gets up and plugs in the
jack for him.*)

CATHY. (*To* SYDNEY, *while* RICHARD *is dialing.*)
Seven girls you interviewed—you told me two.

SYDNEY. I lie.

RICHARD. (*He dials a number, sits on platform.*) Is
Helen there? . . . Oh—and when does she get back?
. . . Not till then? . . . No, no message. (SYDNEY *tries
to figure out for whose benefit the calls are. They are,
of course, for* CATHY'S *who knows it and is imperturb-
able.*) May I speak to Miss Noelle Davis? . . . Hello,
luv, how are you? . . . Alfred Lord Tennyson . . .
Yeah, I got in last night. Listen, what are you doing for
dinner? . . . Get out of it . . . Oh, you'll think of
something. Say you're having an audience with the Pope
. . . There now, you're showing some character. Why
don't you come over here first and then we can go out
to dinner afterwards? . . . Sure, right away. Why not?
. . . Fine. (*He's almost going to hang up.*)

CATHY. (*Helpfully.*) Does she know the address?

RICHARD. (*Glares at* CATHY, *then into phone.*) Hey,
do you know the address? (*Pause.*) What is the address
here?

CATHY. One-twenty-five Jane Street.

RICHARD. One-twenty-five Jane Street. 'Bye. (RICHARD
*hangs up and turns to* CATHY, *faintly victorious and
waiting to see what she'll say.*)

CATHY. It must be a real hardship to have a name
like Noelle.

RICHARD. Oh? Why?

CATHY. Think of all the dreary jokes about the First
Noelle, the Last Noelle—

RICHARD. (*Crosses* L. *and puts telephone on desk.*)
You do take the weight of the whole world upon your
shoulders. (*DOORBELL.*) There's someone at the door.

SYDNEY. (*Who has been watching all of this.*) I'm delighted the two of you have hit it off so well.

CATHY. (*She opens the door to a youngish* MAN.) Hello.

MCFARLAND. Hello. My name is John McFarland. Is there any chance I could talk to Mr. Ford for a few minutes?

RICHARD. I'm Ford—and you're *who?*

MCFARLAND. McFarland. I'm from Time magazine.

RICHARD. I should have known that from the bow-tie. (*To* SYDNEY, *who has stirred.*) You going?

SYDNEY. Yes. (*Seriously.*) Put off that Hollywood trip. Put it off for ten years. And get yourself over to that ceremony on Sunday. (*Quickly, before* RICHARD *can answer.*) Cathy, did we say seven-thirty?

CATHY. (*Has returned to her desk.*) That's right.

(SYDNEY *goes.*)

MCFARLAND. I apologize for bursting in this way. I did call, but first you weren't there and then there was no answer. If you toss me out now I can at least go back to the office and say I saw you. I'll get marks for enterprise.

RICHARD. Well, you've caught me at a bad time, Mr. McFarland. I'm sober. Which means that I have nothing important to say.

MCFARLAND. I'll make allowances for that. Mr. Ford, do you read Time?

RICHARD. It's my Bible.

MCFARLAND. All right, you don't read it. So let me explain. Time tries to cover most of the important books that come out. But every so often we miss one and then we do a review later under a special heading, "Best-Seller Revisited."

RICHARD. You mean we get Time and then we get High-Time.

MCFARLAND. Something like that. But we're running a review of your book next week.

RICHARD. I'm glad you warned me.

MCFARLAND. No, actually it's a good notice. I mean, it's very admiring. I would hope you'd be pleased. I'm here because we want to follow the review with a few personal paragraphs about you.

RICHARD. (*Rises, crosses* L.) What can I tell you? I like a girl that's tall enough to get lipstick on my collar. I prefer to drink Johnnie Walker, but in a pinch I can drink hair tonic. I think the most awesome sight in New York is the men's room at Radio City Music Hall. (*He rattles on, being deliberately baiting, partly to suggest to* MCFARLAND *that he knows this is the sort of thing Time is looking for, partly to get a rise out of Cathy, if possible.* CATHY *remains detached and busy.*) And the advertisements in American magazines are a source of endless wonder and speculation for me. Yesterday I found a very intriguing one. "Remove Unwanted Hair Painlessly." Now think about that. Unwanted hair. Do some people remove wanted hair? What's the matter, you're not taking notes.

MCFARLAND. That's not the kind of piece I want to write.

RICHARD. There's another kind?

MCFARLAND. (*Sits sofa.*) You don't like reporters, do you? I suppose I can understand that. You get gun-shy after a while. Look, I have no "angle." I'm certainly not here to report on your drinking habits. I really admire your work, and I'd like to write something intelligent about it.

RICHARD. I see.

MCFARLAND. Would you say that Gerard Manley Hopkins had some influence on your work?

RICHARD. No.

MCFARLAND. But look. Take a line like "Sun-tipsy, lark-hilarious, tulip-hung, spring jigged on pious February graves." (CATHY's *head has come up at the familiar echo.*) That's a lighter echo of Hopkins.

RICHARD. That's just because the words are hyphenated. Don't you see what that really is? That's not Hopkins. It's Time-style. Don't you hear it? "Pig-eyed, bald-headed, flat-bottomed, average-citizen John Jones. . . ."

CATHY. (*Intervening on* MCFARLAND'S *behalf, and on* RICHARD'S *too.*) Mr. Ford is a little jumpy. He had to get up very early this morning.

RICHARD. Yes, I had to get up very early and meet a deranged person. Not you, Mr. McFarland, of course. But let's get back to Hopkins. Poor old Hopkins. You'd think he never wrote anything but "The Golden Echo." The best things of Hopkins are absolutely direct. (*Quoting.*)

"Margaret, are you grieving
  Over Goldengrove unleaving,
  Leaves, like the things of man, you
  With your new thoughts care for, can you? . . ."

MCFARLAND. (*Correcting him.*)

"You with your *fresh* thoughts care for, can you?"

RICHARD. (*Saying it to himself.*) "You with your . . ." (*Complete change of mood.*) You're right, damn it! And good for you! And I go right to the bottom of the class. It'll teach me to be so bloody patronizing. How did you get to like Hopkins?

MCFARLAND. When I was a sophomore, we had a pro-sem teacher who used to read Hopkins and Eliot and "The Ascent of F 6"—

RICHARD. "The Ascent of F 6." I haven't heard any-one mention that one in years. What's the line I'm try-ing to think of—? (*Quoting.*) "I have read 'Too Late' in the hands of the office clock . . ."

MCFARLAND. (*Picking it up immediately.*) "I have received singular warnings: In the eyes of the beggar I have experienced the earthquake and the simoon. Sitting—" (RICHARD *joins him and they finish it to-gether.*) "—in the crowded restaurant, I have over-heard the confabulation of weasels."

RICHARD. (*Exuberantly.*) The hell with the interview! Let's you and I go out and get drunk and we'll talk about anything in the world but that damn book! (*Crosses upstairs for cap and coat.*)

McFARLAND. (*Cheerfully.*) Sure! Why not?

CATHY. (*Rising, the voice of conscience.*) My, what a short memory we have.

RICHARD. Oh, I have not forgotten you, Miss Shaw! It'll take me at least ten minutes to do that. (*Exits bedroom.*)

CATHY. (*Rises to below stairs.*) I'm not talking about me. You have a date with a Miss Davis, a Miss Noelle Davis.

RICHARD. (*Re-enters.*) Oh, Lord! Listen, call her, will you? The number's there on the pad. Call her and say—

CATHY. But I won't call her. You made a date. I think you should keep it. Anything else would be irresponsible.

RICHARD. (*Comes downstairs.*) You give lessons in etiquette *too?* You know I'd love to mention a subject on which you did not already have an opinion.

CATHY. Well, keep trying. (*To* McFARLAND, *as she goes for her own coat.*) I do hope you'll keep him here until Miss Davis arrives. (*Putting on her coat and gloves.*) I think *I* should go, though. I'll answer these letters and you can sign them in the morning.

RICHARD. Look. Considering your earlier annoucements—why are you so determined that I see Noelle?

CATHY. (*At the door.*) I want you to be able to check off one more thing that won't work. (*To* McFARLAND.) By the way, when she does get here, I do think you should go and leave these two young people together.

(CATHY *leaves. Naturally,* McFARLAND *is looking quizzically at* RICHARD. RICHARD, *after a second of thinking his own thoughts, breaks through it.*)

RICHARD. (*Crosses to kitchen.*) Can I make you a drink? There's some Scotch, I think. (*Hunting some up.*)

McFARLAND. Sure. Thank you. (*Pause, while* RICHARD *is pouring.*) Who is that girl?

RICHARD. (*Turning reflectively, bottle in hand.*) I plan to find out. And when I do—I'll let you know.

*CURTAIN*

# ACT II

*The next morning, about eleven.* RICHARD *is typing.*
*After a moment,* CATHY *enters, though perhaps not*
*as confidently as yesterday.*

CATHY. Well! You're up.

RICHARD. (*Scarcely glancing at her.*) And you're late.

CATHY. (*Getting out of her coat.*) I thought you'd still
be—

RICHARD. You thought! My dear, you think too much.
Such women are dangerous. (*Going right on with his
typing. There is something unusually efficient about him
this morning.*) The idea of a secretary not showing up
until eleven o'clock! Surely that's not the spirit that
made this country great. I've been up since seven. We
have things to do before we clear out of here.

CATHY. Before we clear out of here? For where?

RICHARD. I'll get to that. Find me an envelope, will
you?

CATHY. (*Crosses to desk, doing so, a bit tentatively.*)
I didn't know you could type.

RICHARD. Of course I can type. I can type and I can
fix alarm clocks and make German potato salad. It's
time you noticed. I'm really a Renaissance man.
(*PHONE rings.*) Get that, will you? I'll talk to Sydney.
But if it's anybody else, I'm not here.

CATHY. (*Answering the phone.*) Hello. I'm sorry. Mr.
Ford isn't here. Who's calling please? . . . Oh, Miss
Davis—Miss Noelle Davis. (*She half extends the phone
to* RICHARD, *giving him a chance to change his mind. But
he shakes his head no.*) I'll tell him you called. (*Hangs
up, turns to* RICHARD, *crosses to him.*) I gather that your
evening with Miss Davis was not pure enchantment.

RICHARD. Alas, no. Noelle has changed. She has gone
and tampered with what used to be a breathtaking igno-
rance. I mean, she's been taking courses in the Modern

Novel and has a great many incorrect things to say about John O'Hara. Even that would be bearable, but she insisted upon reading me whole chapters of "Ten North Frederick."

CATHY. (*In sympathy.*) Oh, dear. Oh, *dear.*

RICHARD. Anyway, during the course of this macabre evening, I got to thinking about you.

CATHY. (*Putting on her manner, though we sense she is concelaing some nervousness. In a curious way,* EACH *of them is somewhat different today.*) You mean you kept seeing my face before you—haunting your every dream? (*Crosses* L. *to chair.*)

RICHARD. No, I didn't see your face. I kept hearing your voice. All those simple declarative sentences kept ringing in my ear.

CATHY. Oh really! That must have been rather wearing.

RICHARD. Wearing, but instructive. I would have phoned you last night but I didn't know where to reach you.

CATHY. Phoned me about what?

RICHARD. About us. I just want you to know that I've thought about it and—okay—I agree.

CATHY. Okay to what?

RICHARD. Are you going to get coy on me? Is it possible that you've forgotten everything you said yesterday? (*She doesn't answer.*) Why so silent? Cat got your tongue?

CATHY. I remember what I said yesterday. I also remember that you are rather a raffish fellow, and I don't think I like being made the butt of one of your involved jokes.

RICHARD. If you wish to assume that I'm joking, that's your business. All I can tell you is that I have decided to cooperate with the inevitable.

CATHY. (*Crosses to desk and changes boots for shoes.*) Look, I have a suggestion. Let's do some work first, and you can needle me later.

RICHARD. Needle you? I'm trying to tell you that I

have just been to City Hall, where I discovered what I should have known—that you cannot buy a marriage license unless the lady is present. However, they'll be open till five o'clock, so we have plenty of time.

CATHY. How drunk are you?

RICHARD. (*Crosses* L. *to* CATHY.) Surely you can tell from my steady hand, my level gaze, that I am not drunk. Of course, you're not looking at me at all, so naturally you're missing nuances. (CATHY *crosses* U.R. *with boots and bag.*) In fact, I do wish you would light somewhere. I feel as if I'm conducting a conversation with a bumblebee.

CATHY. (*Sitting in chair and deliberately composing herself.*) All right, I'm here. I'm looking at you. Now please feel free to confide in me.

RICHARD. Yes, but I don't feel free with you sitting there looking so grim.

CATHY. I'm not grim. I'm simply running out of expressions. Surely you have that effect on a lot of people.

RICHARD. All right, are you listening now? I am trying to tell you I've come to the conclusion that you're a girl who is right about everything. Furthermore, when you decide you want something, you get it. I have observed the signs and portents. You have decided to marry me. And I see that the thing for me to do is come quietly. Clearly, I have no alternative. What good would it do even to *try*, when—

CATHY. (*Up.*) Oh, *please* will you stop this? I deserve it, but I find that I'm not enjoying it very much.

RICHARD. Oh? (*Pointing across to the desk.*) If you'll look in the little envelope there that says Trans World Airlines, you'll see that there are two seats for tomorrow night on the five o'clock plane for Los Angeles.

CATHY. You think I'm going to Los Angeles with you?

RICHARD. You know what happens to these marriages where she's in New York and he's in California. It leads to promiscuity, divorce, big telephone bills. We don't want that, do we? (*She says nothing.*) I guess I'll have to go on talking for both of us. You know something?

I'm thirty years old and you are the first lady ever to propose to me. But here's the odd thing. This morning I got another proposal. Now isn't that a coincidence? (*She still doesn't speak.*) All right, you don't think it's a coincidence. But I must tell you about her because you might run into her. She lives just down the street. Her name is Maryrose Cavanaugh and she is seven and a half, going on eight. She was sitting on her front steps in this idiotic spring snow, and I noticed her first of all because she was crying, so I sat down beside her, and I said, "Madam, what is the matter?"

CATHY. (*Because he is waiting for her to say something.*) And what was the matter?

RICHARD. (*Rises, crosses L. of sofa.*) Oh, trouble, trouble, nothing but trouble! Her cat, whose name was Mr. McGregor, had been run over by the milk truck. And her brother Timmy, a lout if ever there was one, had pressed her dolly's eyes, and the eyes had fallen back into the head. I told her she would have to love the dolly twice as much to make it up to her for being blind. Then she started to cry all over again, and she said, "Oh, this is the worst day I've ever *been* to!" Isn't that wonderful? God, for one moment I thought I could write poetry again. Ask me if she proposed immediately.

CATHY. Did she propose immediately?

RICHARD. No! How little you know about women! (*Crosses L. to below stairs.*) She said she hated brown. I said *I* hated brown. She said her mother told her not to eat snow but she ate it all the time. I told her I like to eat snow, too. And then she told me that her sister Vickie, who was mean anyway, broke her arm and it was in a cast. And *she* got a Coke every day and she got sausage for breakfast and new coloring books and presents, and it wasn't fair. Maryrose just didn't see why she couldn't break her arm. And I said I certainly hoped she would break her arm, and that was when she asked me to marry her. And I said I'd be delighted, and how about Christmas-time, but she said she'd have to wait until third grade was over. So that's how we left it. And then I showed her how to make angels. (*Jumping what will probably be her silence.*) Ah! I can see you don't know how to make snow angels! You lie down in the snow and press your head back, and then you waggle your arms up and down. Come on out, and I'll show you— (*Taking her arm and pulling her to her feet.*)

CATHY. (*She explodes and crosses L.*) No, you won't, and will you stop being so bloody charming! There are too many calories for me! I keep feeling like a canary that got caught in a badminton game. You know all these sad books you read about these poor slobs and their problem is they can't communicate? Well, your problem is you communicate too much! You communicate with men, women, children—and I suppose if you were in a tight spot you could probably communicate with inanimate objects! Some morning you should get up and say to yourself, "Today I'm not going to be winning with the elevator boy, or the waitress, or the man with the package. I'm just not going to be adorable at all!" Listen, with the energy you'd save, you could build a cathedral!

RICHARD. Well! And how did I take my finger out of that dyke?

CATHY. (*Crosses L. to desk. Just as quickly subdued now.*) I don't know—but I take it back. What I mean is I wish I didn't say it.

RICHARD. (*Crosses L. to CATHY. Quietly.*) Luv, I would have you know something. There is nothing in this world I am so sick of as the sound of my own voice. Even my very best stories I have heard *so* often. But you're wrong about one thing. All this talking I do is not a form of communication. It's a noise I make to keep people from noticing that I have nothing whatever to say. (*Very slight pause.*) Look, I know where I was last night. Where were you?

CATHY. Why? What difference does it make?

RICHARD. Because something has happened to let the air out. It's really a shame. Think of losing a nerve like yours!

CATHY. I haven't lost anything, thank you.

RICHARD. (*Crosses* C. *on platform.*) But you have. The minute I saw you this morning, and before you said a word, I could see that manner was gone.

CATHY. What manner?

RICHARD. Oh, the lady missionary getting ready to greet the natives. (CATHY *turns so sharply that we suspect she may be in tears and sits in desk chair.*) What's the matter?

CATHY. (*Really at odds with herself.*) What's the matter is—that I feel so *embarrassed*—such a damn fool! I guess I swam out too far.

RICHARD. (*Crosses to* R. *end of sofa.*) Come on, now— you're not going to turn into Little Miss Muffet on me. I liked you better when you were impossible.

CATHY. Yes, but I didn't sleep last night, and I have to have eight hours' sleep or I can't *be* impossible. (*Urgently and helplessly.*) You don't know how I idolized you—idolized you! Why do you suppose I wanted to work for Sydney, particularly? Because he was you publisher. I figured if I was in that office, sooner or later I'd get to meet you.

RICHARD. That's rather sweet.

CATHY. Sweet? Hell, it's idiotic, is what it is! I mean, your books were so real to me that you were real to me. I thought I knew you. What I did was invent a man to match the poetry.

RICHARD. Well, don't look so dismayed. There are no bones broken.

CATHY. No? Are you sure? (*Starts to tidy things up at the desk, as though finishing.*) Look, whether you go to California or stay here in New York, you won't be seeing me again.

RICHARD. (*Sits on sofa.*) Oh?

CATHY. (*Crosses* U.C. *with clipboard.*) Sydney can get you somebody else. (*Forcing herself to face him.*) But I would really like you to believe that I never did anythink like this before. (*Away again.*) Oh, God, I bet you think I write letters to Rock Hudson. (*Crosses* D.C. *with bag and changes from shoes to boots.*) In my whole life, you're the only public person I ever wrote to. No, that's not true; I once wrote a letter to Adlai Stevenson.

RICHARD. You proposed to *him?*

CATHY. No, it was after the election in 1956, and I just said I wished I'd been old enough to vote for him.

RICHARD. Did he answer?

CATHY. Yes, he said *he* wished I'd been old enough to vote for him.

RICHARD. (*Gently kissing her on the top of the head.*) What an idiot child you are.

CATHY. (*In a quick fury.*) Don't, don't! Damn it, if you're going to kiss me, kiss me!

RICHARD. (*Startled, but not for more than a second.*) Certainly.

(RICHARD *kisses her thoroughly, and as they break,* CATHY *makes a little "oooh" sound and leans forward to be kissed again. But at the end of the second kiss, she leaps away, agitated.*)

CATHY. (*Crosses* R. *to sofa.*) What's the matter with me? I must be going out of my mind or something.

RICHARD. Are you upset? Remember, you were the one who—

CATHY. Oh, I was the one, all right. I'm not confused about that.

RICHARD. What are you confused about?

CATHY. I don't like the way I feel. I feel convalescent.

RICHARD. Aren't you exaggerating, just a little bit?

CATHY. (*Crosses* R. *to kitchen and gets glass and container of milk.*) I don't know. I never kissed anybody that way before.

RICHARD. Good heavens! Why not?

CATHY. I guess it just never occurred to me.

RICHARD. It never occurred to you? What are you put together *with?*

CATHY. I don't know. I think I read too much.

RICHARD. (*Trying to conceal his amusement.*) I'm

sure you do. Cathy, right now let me give you some advice. Don't say you love me.

CATHY. Boy! What you need is a little false modesty!

RICHARD. It has nothing to do with me. If you are inexperienced in these matters, you don't know that when you kiss somebody passionately, the pleasure makes you want to say that you love them. And you don't mean it, and later you're sorry.

CATHY. (*Taking a longer look at him.*) Don't be so fatherly and so knowing when you haven't really got the picture at all. The reason I'm at sixes and sevens and eights, the reason I didn't sleep last night—you know, I got up and made cocoa three times?—is because I realized last night—that I could fall in love with you. And I don't think I *like* you. (RICHARD *becomes attentive; she is serious.*) I know I don't approve of you. I don't think it's cute and romantic and colorful that you're throwing your life away, drinking it away, talking it away. I think you're undisciplined. I think you're a slob. (*Puts glass and container in kitchen.*)

RICHARD. (*Crosses* L.) That *is* the party line, but you're not saying it right. You're supposed to say, "Poor Richard—and he's *so* talented."

CATHY. (*Crosses* U.R. *for coat.*) Nothing makes even a dent on you, does it?

RICHARD. For the moment, let's forget about me and examine your behavior. You march in here yesterday and announce that you're going to marry me.

CATHY. (*Crosses to sofa and puts on coat.*) That you were going to marry me.

RICHARD. (*Crosses to below stove.*) Well, it works out to the same thing. Today you come in to say that the deal is off because maybe you're falling in love with me. I would call that very undisciplined behavior. Even slob-like, wouldn't you say?

CATHY. Maybe. (*Sits sofa.*)

RICHARD. It also leads me to believe that you have a very peculiar idea of marriage.

CATHY. (*Too quickly leaping to a prepared position.*)

Well, most of the marriages *I* see are really sort of disgusting!

RICHARD. And where did you get this quaint idea? Were your father and mother unhappily married?

CATHY. My father died when I was four. My mother was happily married five times.

RICHARD. It must have been a problem just keeping up with the monograms on the bath towels.

CATHY. It was more of a problem for me to remember just when Uncle Jack turned into Daddy Jack. No child of mine is ever going to have to call anybody Uncle unless he's an uncle.

RICHARD. Five marriages does seem rather much. One would have thought that after the third she might have dispensed with some of the formalities.

CATHY. That's what I used to say— "Mother, why do you feel you have to go on *marrying* them?" And she said—well, never mind.

RICHARD. (*Sits sofa.*) Oh—go into it.

CATHY. (*Reluctantly.*) She said that marriage was the only place you could say, "Move over—my arm's asleep." (*Looking up, surprised.*) Are you laughing?

RICHARD. I'm thinking she's won her case. That's an unanswerable argument. Now my father had a very different attitude. He used to say, "A man doesn't bury his mistakes, he marries them."

CATHY. Oh, but I believe that! That's why I think you have to be so careful to marry somebody you admire instead of marrying somebody just because you want to *clutch* them, for heaven's sake, and—oh, will you listen to me talk, (*Rises, crosses to chair.*) when it's just five minutes since I was clutching you!

RICHARD. No, it's not, not possible! You're a James M. Barrie character, and what on earth are you doing in this century? It's a cold, cold century, without love and without tenderness, and little girls like you shouldn't be let out of doors. (*He sees tears coming.*) Now wait— you wouldn't, you *wouldn't* cry!

CATHY. (*Crying.*) That's what I thought. (*Fumbling*

*in her purse and fishing out a five-cent package of Kleenex.*) These packages are supposed to be so handy. I don't know what's so handy about them when you can't even get them open! (*And she is still crying.*)

RICHARD. Oh, please stop. You make me feel as if I were drowning puppies. The simplest thing to do would be to put my arm around you. But of course you've made me self-conscious about that.

CATHY. (*Glad to know he's self-conscious.*) Well, that's a step in the right direction!

RICHARD. You know—you have the effect of unsettling me—and I don't like it.

(SYDNEY *enters without knocking, brushing his clothes;* CATHY *and* RICHARD *both jump, startled, speaking in unison.*)

TOGETHER. Oh—Sydney.

SYDNEY. (*Noticing this and staring.*) Well, you both got the name right. What is it you can't place—me? (SYDNEY *now realizes that* CATHY *must have been crying.*) Cathy, are you going someplace?

CATHY. (*Trying to be bright, but concealing nothing, and rattled.*) Oh, Sydney, you know how some days are crazy. (*PHONE.*) I seem to be having an attack of the vapors. (*Crosses to desk. PHONE.*) Hello . . . Oh, yes —when? (*Holding the receiver against her to* RICHARD.) It's your Mr. McFarland—from yesterday—he's written his copy and he has a couple of things to check. Can he come by between six and six-thirty? (RICHARD *nods yes and* CATHY *turns to phone again.*) Yes, that'll be all right. (*Hangs up.*) Now what was I doing? (*To* RICHARD.) Why don't I finish that letter for you?

RICHARD. Because it's just a note to my mother. (*Going to the typewriter, glad enough to give* CATHY *a chance to compose herself.*) I promised to write and let her know whether or not the plane crashed.

(CATHY *hangs up Sydney's coat.* SYDNEY *has a folio of papers with him.*)

SYDNEY. (*Sits sofa.*) Of course, if it crashed she'd see it in the papers.

RICHARD. That's what I said. But she said— (*With a brogue.*) "Sure, Rich, and when do I see the papers?"

SYDNEY. (*Putting a folio he has brought along on the table, aware that* CATHY *is taking the opportunity to improve her face, but chatting easily.*) I didn't know your mother was Irish.

RICHARD. (*Typing.*) That's right. Irish and out of her mind.

SYDNEY. But you like her?

RICHARD. Yes, I do. But I wouldn't want that to become a matter of public gossip. It's so unfashionable. Actually, I had no trouble with my mother after I stopped answering her questions.

SYDNEY. Like for instance?

RICHARD. Oh, she used to say, "Now will somebody kindly tell me what people see in this Miss Brigitte Bardot person?" and I'd *tell* her, and then she'd say, "Rich, you know I don't like that kind of talk." Now I say, "Heaven knows, Mother—heaven knows."

(*PHONE rings.*)

CATHY. (*Picking it up instantly.*) Hello . . . I'm sorry, but Mr. Ford is out at the moment . . . The committee? . . . Oh, New York Hospital . . . About the ceremony tomorrow. (*She glances helplessly at* RICHARD *but he does nothing to rescue her; obviously he is half-listening, though, and bothered by it.*) No, I'm afraid I don't know where he can be reached. He may not be back all day . . . All right, I'll leave a note. (*She hangs up.*)

(*Before anything more can be said,* RICHARD *deflects conversation by spinning in his chair and suddenly reaching for the folio* SYDNEY *has with him;* RICHARD *is jumpier, and trying to conceal it.*)

RICHARD. Sydney! You've brought me a present.

SYDNEY. It's an advance copy of *Look*. They have a four-page spread on "Girl." (RICHARD *lets the folio drop again.*) Don't you want to see it?

RICHARD. No.

CATHY. I want to see it. (*She takes the folio from* SYDNEY.)

RICHARD. I never talked to anybody from *Look*.

SYDNEY. (*While* CATHY *studies it and* RICHARD *moves about, restless and disturbed.*) It's not that kind of piece. Obviously they sent a photographer to Essex and got pictures of the mill house. There's a marvelous shot of that crazy clock tower over the stable. And of course some pictures of Angela. They've captioned it by taking lines from the poems.

CATHY. (*Looking at the folio.*) She was so pretty. (*As though interested in Angela for the first time.*) What did she die of?

RICHARD. (*After a pause, coldly.*) Leukemia.

CATHY. How awful.

RICHARD. It's not a fun disease.

CATHY. Who is she smiling at in this one? Is it—oh, yes, of course, it's you. How long ago was this taken? You seem—

(*She has brought the magazine to him, and now he does take it.*)

RICHARD. It was taken three years ago. (*Reading a caption.*) "Richard Ford, the last of the Romantics. A poet's tender elegy to his dead wife becomes a surprise best-seller." (*He hurls the magazine across the room.*)

(*There is a shocked silence before* SYDNEY *speaks.*)

SYDNEY. What's so terrible about that?

RICHARD. What's so terrible is that I feel like I'm selling her bones.

SYDNEY. If you feel this way, why did you write it?

RICHARD. Sydney, those poems were exercises. Busy

work. It's what I did instead of blowing the top of my head off.

SYDNEY. Then why did you let me publish it?

RICHARD. Because I wasn't thinking. And even if I was, how could I have dreamt it would turn into this—this—

SYDNEY. Success. Is that the dirty word you're trying to avoid? (*Nerving himself to the moment.*) Richard—

RICHARD. (*Exasperated.*) No, Sydney! Before you start over, I am not going to that ceremony tomorrow.

SYDNEY. Then you didn't hear anything I said?

RICHARD. I heard everything you said. The mistake you make is—is—

SYDNEY. What is the mistake I make?

RICHARD. You think because you know all the facts, you know the truth. It doesn't necessarily follow. (*DOORBELL.*) Who's that?

SYDNEY. I think I know. (SYDNEY *has gone to the door and opens it to* GINNY, *Angela's sister. She is a straightforward girl in her early thirties, impeccably dressed.* SYDNEY *embraces her.*) Well, hello, Ginny. You're looking very glamorous for this early in the day.

(*They cross* D.C. *on platform.*)

GINNY. Oh, I'm doing all right for a middle-aged lady of thirty-five. Actually, I'm thirty-six. Why do I lie for just one year?

(*She has turned to look for* RICHARD. *As their eyes meet, there is a brief moment of strained silence, of stiffness. Then* RICHARD *goes to her.*)

RICHARD. Hello, Ginny.

GINNY. Hello, Richard.

RICHARD. It's—something of a surprise to see you. How did you know I was here? (*He is very restrained.*)

SYDNEY. I told her you were here.

RICHARD. I see.

SYDNEY. (*As much to relieve the oddly charged atmosphere as anything, introducing* CATHY.) This is Miss Shaw. And this is Richard's sister-in-law, Mrs. Baker.

CATHY. How do you do?

GINNY. Hello.

SYDNEY. Ginny, will you forgive me if I have to bolt right out of here—I go through life being a half-hour late for everything, but today I'm up to forty-five minutes.

GINNY. (*Giving him a manila envelope.*) Sure Sydney —run along. Oh, listen, Mother insisted I give you these. Like really insisted. If you want my opinion, it's a crazy idea.

SYDNEY. That's perfectly all right. She told me about it. I'll be delighted to read them.

RICHARD. Goodbye, Sydney.

(SYDNEY *exits.*)

GINNY. Richard, I thought maybe I could see you alone.

CATHY. I can go upstairs—

RICHARD. (*To* CATHY.) Please. (*To* GINNY.) Miss Shaw is an old and trusted employee, privy to all my secrets.

GINNY. (*Crosses* R. *to sofa. Taking a fresh and markedly curious look at* CATHY. *She is not one to miss possibilities.*) She may be trusted, but she's not very old.

RICHARD. (*Crosses to* C. *of sofa. Formally, with detachment.*) And how is your family, Ginny?

GINNY. (*Sits sofa.*) Well, John has given up smoking and he's impossible. The baby has the virus and Billy got fifty-nine in Latin. I mean everything is absolutely routine. And how are you? Mother and Dad always thought they'd hear from you.

RICHARD. About what?

GINNY. About anything. Even that little maid you had at the mill house—remember Rosie? She sent them a Christmas card.

RICHARD. Ginny, would you like a drink?

GINNY. Thank you, no. I'm still getting over last night. It was one of those times where I had one for the road. And then I had four for the road. Though I gather I'm not in it with you.

RICHARD. (*Crosses* U.C. *for drink from chest.*) Evidently not. Because I'm going to have one.

GINNY. What's the matter? You seem feverish or something.

RICHARD. What I seem is slightly in my cups for the good reason that I am slightly in my cups.

GINNY. No you're not. I think I know what it is. It disturbs you to see me. I look a *little* bit like Angela. You know, I don't think about Angela much any more. Isn't that terrible? But just now I had a sudden image of the last time I saw the two of you together. It was in that hotel in Cannes, remember? She was wearing a yellow dress with huge pockets. She seemed so happy that night. So alive!

RICHARD. Why do people say that?

GINNY. What?

RICHARD. She seemed so alive. Everybody who's alive seems alive. I wait for the day when somebody says, "Good old George—strange that he's gone. He always seemed so dead."

GINNY. What is this? What are you being so sensitive about? Two years later I can't mention my own sister without your snapping at me.

RICHARD. I didn't mean to snap at you and you may mention anything you wish to mention.

GINNY. It doesn't feel that way. I feel a wall of restraint. What's caused this—your new celebrity?

RICHARD. Yes, I'm a big man now and I speak only to bartenders. Ginny, if you want to talk about this hospital thing, there's no point. I'm not going. Did Sydney ask you to come?

GINNY. No.

RICHARD. Your mother?

GINNY. No, I am not a messenger girl. Nobody sent

me. I'm here on my own. I thought you ought to know the situation.

RICHARD. What situation?

GINNY. Dad hasn't been well lately. I think maybe he's dying. And mother's kind of in pieces. What's kept her together is this hospital business. I mean she can fight with the architect and that cheers her up a little. The point is that these are two old people. This is very important to them. I think it's inconsiderate of you not to be there.

RICHARD. You think my presence lends grace to every occasion?

GINNY. (*A little human explosion.*) Do you think *I* want to be there when they cut the ribbons and make all those boring speeches? You're not an obtuse person. Why are you pretending to be? You had to write those poems. That was your own private memorial to Angela. And God knows they've been admired enough. You've read the clippings.

RICHARD. I haven't read them.

GINNY. Don't you see this is their turn? This is their public memorial to Angela . . . Why won't you have any part of it?

RICHARD. Because I can't.

GINNY. Surely you don't hold it against mother that you two quarreled in the beginning. That's all over. She has no malice. You know she said something very sweet about the book. She said, I know the book will last a lot longer than the hospital.

RICHARD. I don't know, I'd say the hot money was on the hospital.

GINNY. (*Looking sharply at* RICHARD.) I thought you were being sentimental about Angela. It's worse than that. You're sentimental about yourself. I think you should stop playing Hamlet.

RICHARD. Is that what I'm playing?

GINNY. Look, I always respected you. I always thought you were special. But right from the beginning, I never quite trusted you.

RICHARD. I knew that.

GINNY. There was something about your attitude. For instance, I used to think you deliberately mussed your hair before you came to dinner.

RICHARD. But I was so charming with my hair mussed.

GINNY. It was a pose. You are a great one for taking poses.

RICHARD. (*Becoming unsettled.*) Ginny, you want to go back and poke around in the ashes. But I cannot, I will not!

GINNY. I'd say when you wrote those poems you had quite a little revel in the ashes.

RICHARD. (*Angry.*) That's what you'd say, is it?

GINNY. Most people pretend to be cheerful. I think you pretend to be suffering. Okay, you're a troubled genius, and you haven't had a happy day or a sober one since Angela died. But I want to say something. Maybe I didn't see you much after you were married, but I was there in the beginning when you were going with Angela. How come I didn't get any sense of the fireworks? I was there on the day you were married and I never had any feeling it was the beginning of Tristan and Isolde! What's vulgar about the book—what's all wrong about you, is that you're trying to dramatize something that never existed at all!

CATHY. (*She jumps up and into the fray, unable to contain herself any longer.*) How dare you come in and talk to him like this! You don't know how he feels. You don't know what he's been through. You shouldn't say another word!

RICHARD. (*Wheeling on* CATHY, *cutting her down.*) *You* shouldn't say another word! You will *not* put your nose into matters you know nothing whatever about! Ginny, I didn't mean—

(CATHY *recoils, stung.*)

GINNY. (*Quickly ending the discussion.*) Your little friend is right. I have gone past the decent limits, I'm sorry. I still think you should come to the ceremony. You have come half the distance—and now you must come the other half. I'll go now and you have a couple of stiff drinks and forget about me. (*Again a curious, wondering look.*) Goodbye, Miss Shaw.

(*She goes.* RICHARD *half-follows her to the door, then turns to Cathy.* CATHY *is faced away, humiliated.*)

RICHARD. I drink so much—why do I never get drunk? Cathy, I know you're hurt. I know you're humiliated. But you had no business interrupting. (*Crosses to below* C. *of sofa.*)

CATHY. (*Turning and flaring.*) I never wanted to sit here while you talked to her! You made me sit here! She's such a stupid girl!

RICHARD. (*Firmly.*) No, she is not. She is a perfectly intelligent girl. And she knows a thing or two more than you do.

CATHY. (*Crosses* C. *on platform.*) Then why did she behave the way she did? What did she think she was getting at? Lord, she made it sound as if you didn't love Angela.

RICHARD. I didn't love her.

CATHY. (*Stunned.*) I don't believe you.

RICHARD. (*Slight pause.*) But you do believe me or you wouldn't look so horrified.

CATHY. (*Groping as she tries to readjust.*) If you didn't love her, why did you marry her?

RICHARD. Because she was there. Because I'm a bastard. Because I was desperate.

CATHY. Why were you so desperate?

RICHARD. (R. *of sofa.*) I was working in a paint and wallpaper store. My idea of hell is an eternity spent in a paint and wallpaper store. I was at the store until six and writing at night. Or trying to write. But the worst thing, the intolerable thing was that I was beginning to lose that little comforting feeling that I was really a genius, see?, and the world was waiting.

CATHY. (*Sits* L. *end of sofa.*) But that doesn't make any sense at all. "The Apprentice" was out by that time.

RICHARD. Yes, that came out to a great burst of apathy. And, unlike Scott Fitzgerald, I woke up one morning to find myself obscure.

CATHY. So immediately you started looking for a girl with money.

RICHARD. (*Crosses* L. *to below stairs.*) No. I wasn't smart, I was lucky. I met Angela quite by accident. In those days I used to spend every Sunday at the National Gallery because there was no place in our flat to write. Also, I had to get away from the beaded lamp shades in the living room and in every bedroom there was a copy of the Return from Calvary. My mother figured you didn't go to heaven unless you died under a copy of the Return from Calvary. Anyway, I was in the tearoom of the National Gallery when I saw this blond girl. She had a book. And the book was "The Apprentice." I kept staring at her like a nut. You understand that there were only about thirty copies sold in all of London, and the chances of my running into one—well, there was no chance. Eventually I said in this loud voice—loud because I was nervous and felt such a fool—"Miss, that's my book. May I autograph it for you?"

CATHY. Well, I wouldn't let anyone pick me up that way.

RICHARD. (*Crosses to* L. *of chair.*) Well, she wondered whether or not she should call for help—I had such a wild look. So that's how we met. It turned out that her father had rented a castle outside London for the summer. He would have preferred Buckingham Palace, but it wasn't available. No, I'm not being fair. Actually, he was rather kindly. Saint Martin getting ready to share his cloak with a beggar. But her mother always seemed to be looking at me through an invisible lorgnette. It was as if she knew I'd just come out of prison having committed some unmentionable sex crime.

CATHY. And Angela?

RICHARD. Well, you see, she thought I was going to be a great poet.

CATHY. (*Crosses* L. *to above chair.*) You can be.

RICHARD. Absolutely. But I didn't know she was falling in love with me, really. She seemed so cool and detached. She was so perfect, in this spun-glass way, I used to wonder if anything could cause a ripple on that millpond.

CATHY. Did anything—ever?

RICHARD. (*Crosses* C. *on platform.*) Oh, yes. I asked her out as often as I dared. And we'd drive to the movies in her snow-white Bentley. Or walk in the park. Then, the summer was over, and the Howards were going back to New York. And that Sunday she said she wanted to go back to the Tower of London. We were outside in the courtyard, and I was showing her that stone block where Lady Jane Grey was beheaded, and I noticed there were tears in her eyes and I thought she was thinking about poor Lady Jane Grey—and suddenly she took my hand and said, "Richard, I can't go home with them. I can't leave you. I'll die, I'll really die." I still remember the way my heart hammered. And I didn't think, She loves me, she loves me. I thought—This is it—this is my chance, my way out—my Fullbright. And I asked her to marry me.

CATHY. I don't believe you were as calculating as that.

RICHARD. I was precisely as calculating as that. I thought my talent was more important than anybody or anything in this world.

CATHY. And you never thought you were doing an injustice to Angela? . . .

RICHARD. No.

CATHY. . . . Or even to yourself?

RICHARD. No! I've told you No! (CATHY *sits chair;* RICHARD *crosses* R. *and sits* R. *end of sofa.*) Well—once, just before we were married, I had a pang. I was coming home in the bus and there was this couple facing me. He looked like nothing in particular. And she was really homely. She had one of those faces that's all mouth and teeth—like when you look at yourself in the back of a spoon. Also, she was wearing glasses, and she took them off and—almost as if she weren't thinking—she leaned over and polished them on the knees of his trousers. And he looked at her with such—such passion that I felt really envious. I went home and called up Angela. I don't know what I was going to say—but I was going to say something. I told her I had to see her. And she said come over to dinner. And then in the background I heard her mother's voice saying, "Ask him if he has another suit."

CATHY. And so you were married.

RICHARD. (*Picks up copy of Look.*) And lived happily ever after, or so it says in all the magazines. What irony —what penance for my sins that I have fallen into a legend.

CATHY. Then who was the girl?

RICHARD. What girl?

CATHY. The other girl, the girl in the poems.

RICHARD. There is no other girl.

CATHY. But there has to be, otherwise the whole thing's a fake.

RICHARD. (*Crosses L. of table.*) That's right. The book's a fake, and I'm a fake.

CATHY. Oh, but it does not *feel* fake!

RICHARD. Don't tell me what it feels like. I'm telling you what it is. Now shall I bend down and pick up your shattered illusions?

CATHY. What do you want me to say?

RICHARD. Don't say anything. Marry me.

CATHY. Please. You've made enough jokes about that.

RICHARD. No, the games are over. I mean it. Marry me, be with me, stay with me. I'm drowning, Cathy. I'm in a room without doors. I was going to say that I have no hope, but it's worse than that: I have no preferences. It makes no difference to me whether I'm in New York or in London. Everything is the *same* shade of grey.

CATHY. How would I help?

RICHARD. You're real, you still believe in things.

CATHY. And you don't?

RICHARD. No, but I believe that you believe. There's guilt by association. Maybe there's innocence by association.

CATHY. (*Troubled.*) No, Richard, I can't. I'm sorry— I'm truly sorry—but no, I can't. I just can't.

RICHARD. (*Gently.*) Luv—don't look so frightened and so upset. I understand. In effect, I am asking you to step into my nightmare. Why would you? Why should you?

CATHY. Oh, no, it's not that. It's not what you think. It's—it's—

RICHARD. It's what?

CATHY. (*Forcing herself to think through exactly what dismays her.*) See—I would expect that eventually you'd love me.

RICHARD. Eventually maybe I would.

CATHY. No. If you didn't love her, you won't love anybody. (*She waits for an answer.*) You don't say anything.

RICHARD. No, I don't. Why is that, do you suppose?

CATHY. (*Suddenly terribly unsettled, and feeling that she has failed everything.*) Richard, don't look that way!

RICHARD. What way?

CATHY. You look so *departed*—as if you'd just gone and left yourself. I'm sorry I can't be of help to you. But it wouldn't do. It wouldn't do.

RICHARD. You know, you're not really entitled to that attitude.

CATHY. Why not?

RICHARD. You think love isn't necessary.

CATHY. (*Looking at him.*) And you think it isn't possible. (*Very slight pause.*) What if we're both wrong?

(*She moves toward him, hesitantly. Then he moves swiftly and they embrace.*)

### THE CURTAIN FALLS

# ACT III

*After twilight, the same day.* CATHY *is sitting alone, in near darkness, as* SYDNEY *lets himself in.*

SYDNEY. Cathy—you there? (*Sees her.*) What are you doing here alone in the dark?

CATHY. Sitting.

SYDNEY. (*Starting to light the LAMPS.*) I would have been through long ago, but Joe Carlin caught me as I was half out the door. And of course I had to listen to a long song and dance about his book. He doesn't like the cover design, his wife doesn't like the cover design, his girl doesn't like the— (*With the LIGHTS on, getting a good look at her.*) Hey, what's with you?

CATHY. Nothing. But I'm glad you came. I want to try out my voice.

SYDNEY. You want to what?

CATHY. I want to hear how I sound. I think maybe I'm drunk. I hope I'll sound cute and funny, like Shirley McLaine in the movies.

SYDNEY. What are you drinking?

CATHY. I don't know, but it's awful sweet.

SYDNEY. (*Inspecting the bottle.*) Cointreau. And you've got it in a waterglass? You're going to be sick.

CATHY. You're so right.

SYDNEY. Where's your coat? We'd better get you out in the air.

CATHY. I'm not sure I can move. Maybe I should have some coffee first, or a glass of milk. I don't know— something.

SYDNEY. (*Seeing a coffee pot still plugged in.*) Do you suppose there's anything left in this? Yes, there is. (*Pouring some, and finally asking the obvious question.*) By the way, where has our friend Richard disappeared to?

CATHY. I don't know. There was this little puff of smoke, and whoosh—he was gone.

56

SYDNEY. (*Bringing her a cup of coffee.*) Well, he has one hell of a nerve to be feeding you liquor.

CATHY. He wasn't feeding me anything. This was all self-service, cafeteria style. I've been having a little do-it-yourself orgy. (*Has pronounced it correctly, but wonders.*) It isn't or-gee, is it? (*Points to the packet* SYDNEY *has dropped on the desk when he came in.*) What did that Mrs. Baker give you?

SYDNEY. Some letters from Angela. Her mother thought there might be a book in them.

CATHY. Is there?

SYDNEY. I just glanced at them while I was waiting for the car, and they're charming as Angela was charming. But that doesn't make a book.

CATHY. Sydney, old sport, tell me what makes a book, because I have this keen plot about this dizzy girl who somehow or other—

(*Suddenly her cup clatters down against the saucer.* SYDNEY *notices.*)

SYDNEY. What's the matter?

CATHY. Oh, Sydney, I feel like a dropped watch.

SYDNEY. I see that. Are you falling in love with him?

CATHY. (*Evading it now.*) This coffee is so bitter. It tastes like something you should put on scratches.

SYDNEY. (*Insisting.*) *Are* you?

CATHY. (*Giving up.*) I guess so. I keep writing his name with my finger. I want him to whisper to me.

SYDNEY. (*Pale.*) And you would tell me that?

CATHY. You asked me, Sydney—twice.

SYDNEY. But surely you understood how much I *did not* want to hear it.

CATHY. Sydney, darling Sydney — I'm sorry — I didn't—

SYDNEY. (*Regretting his break, and in charge of himself again.*) Of course you didn't. And please don't be sorry. And whatever you do, don't encourage me into self-pity. I consider that the most unlovely of all human emotions. (*Directly.*) So you're in love with him. How does he feel?

CATHY. He doesn't feel anything. Anything at all—about anything.

SYDNEY. Don't fool yourself.

CATHY. No. I'm not fooling myself. He's not really present. When I'm with him, I have the same feeling I had when I saw the Parthenon last summer. What's left is so remarkable that you keep thinking how wonderful it must have been when it was all there.

SYDNEY. That's ungrateful of you. And not a very good analogy. People come from all over the world just to see what's left of the Parthenon.

CATHY. I guess. Anyway, it doesn't matter. He doesn't love me. Do you know something? He didn't even love Angela.

SYDNEY. (*Startled, but not taking long to answer.*) Rubbish.

CATHY. No, he told me himself. He married her for her money.

SYDNEY. Is that what he says? Well, this has been a day of revelations. Do you want some more coffee?

CATHY. No, I want my coat. I want to get out of here. He'll be back, and I just couldn't bear to see him again. Oh God, I wish I'd never met him. (*She has got to her feet.*)

SYDNEY. (*Swiftly picking up her coat and helping her with it.*) Don't be so alarmed. These sudden infatuations are like summer storms. They're very noisy, but they're not really so dangerous.

CATHY. You mean I'll get over it? Even so, everything is changed.

SYDNEY. How changed?

CATHY. It's like I've seen him in color, and now I'll go all the rest of my life seeing everybody else in black and white.

SYDNEY. (*Concealing his pain and concentrating on helping her.*) How many buttons does this coat have?

CATHY. (*Suddenly.*) Sydney, this is terrible. I'm a disgrace. But I have to lie down. For a minute. For just one minute. Oh, dear—oh, dear—

SYDNEY. That's all right. Go on, *lie* down. I'll get that afghan to put over you. (*He turns his back to look for the afghan and* CATHY *makes a sudden, surprising bolt for the stairs up to the bedroom.* SYDNEY *turns.*) Where are you going?

CATHY. (*Halfway up stairs.*) He's not going to come in and find me right here—passed out cold! (*She hurries on up, unsteady but determined.*)

SYDNEY. (*After her.*) Listen, you are in no shape to climb up to that tree house—!

CATHY. Yes, I am. (*Falters and* SYDNEY *catches up with her.*) Oh, people who drink are so brave. Think of feeling this way *often.*

(SYDNEY *gets her into the room. As he is returning without the afghan,* RICHARD *lets himself in. They are* BOTH *surprised for a moment.*)

RICHARD. Where's—?
SYDNEY. She's lying down.

(RICHARD *reflects for a second, then dismisses his query and with some determination picks up an attaché case in a corner, goes to the desk, and begins stuffing mail and several books into it.* SYDNEY *watches him, silent. Finally* RICHARD *speaks.*)

RICHARD. What happened?
SYDNEY. She was drinking Cointreau out of a waterglass—with predictable results.
RICHARD. (*Hangs up cap and coat.*) Is she all right? Can we do anything?
SYDNEY. She'll be all right.
RICHARD. I didn't think she drank.
SYDNEY. She doesn't.
RICHARD. (*Crosses to desk and turns on LAMP.*) I suppose you think it's my bad example.

SYDNEY. What I think is so complicated that I don't believe I want to go into it. But I do have a theory about *your* drinking. I think you talk more about it than you drink.

RICHARD. You mean I'm a secret non-drinker. (*Opens suitcase and begins to pack.*)

SYDNEY. What did go on around here? Why was Cathy upset?

RICHARD. Sydney, I'm something of a mess. So, naturally, my relationships reflect that.

SYDNEY. What's the suitcase for?

RICHARD. My clothes. I had my ticket changed. I'm taking the midnight plane.

SYDNEY. To California?

RICHARD. (*Nodding.*) All of a sudden I'm tired of New York. I find the tall buildings oppressive. And there's too much glass everywhere. Have you noticed that?

SYDNEY. Richard, I feel obliged to talk you out of this trip.

RICHARD. Why?

SYDNEY. Because Hollywood is a dump heap for writers like you. I see the end of this road. Pretty soon I will be getting funny letters about the days you spend around the pool and the nights you sat up writing lousy dialogue for a Sandra Dee movie. And then you'll be replaced on the Sandra Dee movie, and after a while even the letters won't be so funny.

RICHARD. What nonsense! Sydney, why do you always talk in absolutes?

SYDNEY. Because I am interested in absolutes. I hate to see a man as indecisive as you are, because when you're that indecisive you make a lot of wrong decisions.

RICHARD. Sydney, you should write a book. You know that. You owe it to us all. Either write a book or stop sounding like a fourth-century Chinese philosopher. You know, I never had trouble packing until I bought a second pair of shoes.

SYDNEY. Is it possible, Richard—is it really possible that you think you didn't love Angela?

RICHARD. (*Wheeling on him, furious, though trying to conceal it.*) Does little Miss Shaw keep *anything* to herself?

SYDNEY. My God, Richard! I knew you both and it's not in any way relevant *why* you married her or *how* it began or whether—

RICHARD. Sydney. *Please* will you not go into it?

SYDNEY. I will go into it! I want to tell you something. It's come to the point where this word "love" makes me want to vomit. There is no subject in the world about which there is so much confusion, so much misunderstanding, so much plain slop! Our generation isn't looking for love. We're looking for desperation. We think it isn't real unless we have fever of a hundred and three. I tell you, to love—is to cherish, to care for, to comfort, to be one with—and, dammit, I tell you you loved your wife!

RICHARD. Sydney, you are wasting your breath. I was *there*. Sure, sure, a lot of things you say make sense to me now. But now is too late. You cannot love retroactively.

SYDNEY. You mean you never, ever felt *anything* at the time?

RICHARD. Oh, I felt a lot of things. I think of that awful April when she was dying. And of course, she knew. It's only in the movies that they don't know. And she was very brave, and I was— (*Curtly.*) I was a blank. I divided my time more or less equally between small bars and large churches. I could have faced her suffering, I think. But it took courage to face her bravery. One afternoon—it was just a couple of days before she died —she put her hand in mine. But she kept the hand in a little fist, and I knew it was because she didn't want me to see that the fingers were just bones. And I thought, I have always loved this woman. You know I could have believed that?

SYDNEY. Why didn't you?

RICHARD. Because Angela didn't. I could have fooled myself, but I couldn't fool her.

SYDNEY. You're sure?

RICHARD. Practically the last thing she said to me in this world—she said, "Richard, when I am dead, you are going to be relieved. Now promise me you won't feel guilty about that." (SYDNEY *is silent, and* RICHARD *takes his silence for confirmation.*) That does rather end the discussion, doesn't it? (*Working to change the subject.*) Do you know that poem of Auden's that begins "Stay with me, Ariel, while I pack"?

SYDNEY. (*Thinking his own thoughts. In a moment he sits down near the desk, observing* RICHARD *in a new light.*) I'm not sure that I do.

RICHARD. I never open a suitcase that I don't think of it. It's quite a perfect line. It's simple, almost colloquial, and yet it's poetry. "Stay with me, Ariel, while I pack. . . ."

SYDNEY. I'll stay with you, Ariel. But the poetry I'd like to discuss is your poetry. All along I sensed there was something peculiar in your reaction to this book. I thought it was because you didn't like the title.

RICHARD. Naturally I don't like the title.

SYDNEY. Well, I sent you three cables and eventually we had to call it something. Would you have been happier if we'd called it "Further Poems," or "Poems, 1964"?

RICHARD. Sydney, nothing would make me happy about that book. I have done the one thing I thought I would never do. I have used the language to deceive.

SYDNEY. Oh, for God's sake—

RICHARD. No, let me finish. See, I believe in words. I think when they're put together they should mean something. They have an exact meaning, a precise meaning. There is more precision in one good sonnet than there is in an Atlas Missile. Do you understand I've gone all my life trying to elbow my way into a society that seemed always to be saying "If you don't understand it, it must be marvelous"? Whereas I think if you don't understand it, there's something the matter with the writer. I don't trust a poem that needs footnotes. I demand more from a writer than I do from a painter. If a painter wants to dribble six shades of blue on the canvas and call it an abstraction, I may or may not like it—but I won't feel betrayed, because *blue* doesn't mean anything.

SYDNEY. And you think the words in your poems don't mean anything?

RICHARD. (*Shouting.*) Aren't you listening to me at all? Of course the words mean something! Pick up any magazine, read any review! Any fool can tell you what my poems mean! They mean I was a devoted husband and that ours was the love-match of the century!

SYDNEY. If you're going to be so heated, and wave your hands about, you shouldn't smoke. You're dropping ashes all over your clothes.

RICHARD. It's all right. It keeps the moths away.

SYDNEY. (*Quietly.*) You won't believe this, but you are sentimental about yourself.

RICHARD. No, I won't believe that.

SYDNEY. That's because you've forgotten the meaning of the word. It means an emotion that's out of touch with reality.

RICHARD. (*Bored.*) It's good to know that. (*Goes on with his packing.*)

SYDNEY. To go absolutely ga-ga about a French poodle is sentimental because it's in excess—it's out of proportion. You see that. But do you see that you're being sentimental when you despise yourself this much?

RICHARD. (*He will not be drawn into this.*) Do you want to hand me that pile of shirts? And let's get those damn cardboards out of there.

SYDNEY. (*Obliging, without letting up.*) Okay. Let me ask you something else. You're so hopped up on the meaning of words. I gather that Milton means something definite, and Matthew Arnold. What about the rest of us ordinary mortals? Do our words have meaning?

RICHARD. You're damn right they do. And when you write a note to the laundry and say, "No starch, *please.*" you do not mean that you are in general dissatisfied with the appearance of your shirts. You mean no starch.

SYDNEY. (*Satisfied. This has brought him to the point he's been working toward. He goes to the packet on the desk and opens it.*) We're agreed. Now I want to read you something that seems to me to have only one possible meaning. It's a letter.

RICHARD. Mail it to me.

SYDNEY. I'm going to read it to you. I want you to listen to all of it.

RICHARD. (*Irritable, still packing.*) All of it, what do you mean all of it? How long is it?

SYDNEY. (*Has thumbed through the letters to find what he wants.*) It's only half a page. I just don't want you to interrupt.

RICHARD. (*Exasperated.*) Look, Sydney. I can hardly interrupt if you won't even get started.

SYDNEY. It's dated January 5, 1962, and it begins— (*Reading, carefully keeping any of the letter's emotional inflections out of his voice but clearly following its thought.*) "Dear One. Your letter today was almost as good as a visit with you. I swear I heard your croaky laugh, and I know I felt your hand on my shoulder. About the other—my darling, what shall I tell you? The doctor says I look better every day, and I say, 'Doctor, I *feel* better,' and he's a liar and I'm a liar."

RICHARD. (*Fiercely.*) Stop it—stop it!

SYDNEY. (*Calmly.*) Yes, it's from Angela to her father, and you are not going to interrupt.

RICHARD. Sydney, I won't—!

SYDNEY. (*More quietly still, measuring each word.*) You are *not going to interrupt*. (*Continues reading.*) "All my life I've been late for everything. It's like me to be so slow about dying. There. Does that word frighten you, my dearest? It mustn't. There are worse things. Just pray it be soon. It must be soon, if only for my darling Richard. He suffers more than I do. He hovers over me, looking like a ravaged archangel. Always between us, and always unspoken, is the question: How can I leave him when he loves me so? Oh, Lord, how dear he is, how good he is—"

(RICHARD *has crossed the room and ripped the letter
out of* SYDNEY'S *hands. He stands still, reading the
rest of it. Then he puts it down on the desk. The
only hint we get of how moved he is comes from
the way he places his hand, palm-down, on the
letter.* SYDNEY *is silent.* RICHARD, *finally realizing
he must speak, seizes on something irrelevant—the
signature on the letter.*)

RICHARD. Angie. . . . I had forgotten that her father
called her Angie. Nobody else did.

SYDNEY. I know.

RICHARD. (*Fighting to keep his tone casual.*) Actually,
I never called her Angela. I called her Kaasi.

SYDNEY. Kaasi?

RICHARD. In Dutch it means "little cheese." It started
out as a joke because she liked cheese. (*He stops abruptly and turns sharply away from* SYDNEY, *with his
back to us. The emotional impact of what he has heard
has reached him and we know he is struggling to control
himself.*) My head is making so much noise I can't
think. (*Goes to the window.*) I wonder if we can open
this window a little bit. (*He opens it and takes a breath
of air.*) Even with the snow you can feel it's April.

(*The DOORBELL rings.* SYDNEY *is instantly on his feet,
to protect* RICHARD. *He opens the door, not all the
way, to* McFARLAND.)

McFARLAND. Oh—hello—

SYDNEY. I'm sorry. Mr. Ford isn't seeing anyone.

McFARLAND. (*A bit flustered by whatever he hears in*
SYDNEY'S *voice.*) Oh. I did call earlier. Well, then, could
I leave these with you—? (*Starts to hand* SYDNEY *a few
pages of notes.*)

RICHARD. (*His head comes up sharply.*) McFarland?
(SYDNEY *turns from the door.* RICHARD *now comes to
them, swiftly, impulsively, seizing on the intrusion and
speaking almost without interruption.*) Come in, come on

in! I don't think you two know each other. Sydney Carroll, this is John McFarland. And, Sydney, I want you to take special note of Mr. McFarland. Do not be deceived by that sport jacket. Mr. McFarland belongs to that dying breed that still reads poetry. And he quotes Hopkins correctly. And yesterday he put me in my place so properly that I shall be polite to reporters for all the rest of the month. And—let me see what else— (*He is running out of steam, a bit fevered.*)

McFARLAND. (*Aware that some situation exists.*) Look—I sense that I have arrived at exactly the wrong moment. Why don't I leave these here, and your secretary can make the corrections and get them back to me.

RICHARD. No, it's all right. Really it's all right. Do sit down. (*During this,* RICHARD *is plainly wrestling with himself, using* McFARLAND *as release.*)

McFARLAND. (*Suddenly remembering, and pulling it out of his coat pocket.*) Oh, I brought you that book we were talking about yesterday.

RICHARD. You did? That was good of you. People who promise to send you money nearly always remember. But nobody ever remembers they promised to send you a book.

SYDNEY. And a good thing, too. People should *buy* books. Remember that.

McFARLAND. This isn't so easy to get hold of. It's out of print.

SYDNEY. (*Reaching for it.*) What is it?

RICHARD. "The Stuffed Owl." You've heard of it.

McFARLAND. It's a collection of very bad poems by well-known writers. A sort of Leaden Treasury of English Verse. I guess the editor thought it would be fun to find out how bad a good poet can get.

SYDNEY. (*Leafing it, half an eye on Richard.*) Oh, yes—

RICHARD. Well, now! And what did you want to check?

McFARLAND. Look, I try not to take up time with simple biographical facts that can be checked anywhere

But I've been through our files and the public library, and I have here a wonderland of conflicting information —most of which, I imagine, came directly from you. (*With a grin.*) It is variously reported that you were an orphan and your father was a camel driver, and your mother played the leading man in a Christmas pantomime, and you were brought up by an uncle who printed money in the basement.

RICHARD. I like that.

McFARLAND. Now I don't doubt you ran away to sea at fourteen, and worked on a whaling station, but were you ever a walk-on in "Aida" at the Met?

RICHARD. (*To* SYDNEY.) You see why my books are so slim. My best work has gone into interviews. My father was and is a night watchman at Harrods. The only job I ever had was in a paint and wallpaper store. (*Abruptly.*) And what do you really want to know?

McFARLAND. (*Looking up quickly, catching* RICHARD's *shift of tone.*) Why do you think I have something else to ask you?

RICHARD. Because those questions were much too routine to bring you all the way down here after hours.

McFARLAND. I was working up to it gradually. I guess I was too gradual. (*Not exactly easy, because he senses he is on touchy ground.*) But here's the thing. Your refusal—or at least your reluctance—to talk about the book has led to some—speculation. Some mystery.

RICHARD. Oh?

McFARLAND. (*Making himself ask the question.*) Were—the poems written for "Girl" written at different times—or were they all written after—?

RICHARD. (*Straightforwardly.*) They were all written in the three months after my wife died.

McFARLAND. (*Getting up.*) That's it. And thank you very much. (*He extends his hand.*)

RICHARD. (*Shaking his hand.*) You're welcome. It was a pleasure to meet you—and something of a surprise.

McFARLAND. (*Smiling and meaning it.*) The same to you. (*To* SYDNEY.) Good night.

SYDNEY. (*Over his shoulder; he is still leafing the book.*) Good night. (MCFARLAND *leaves.* RICHARD *has gone up to the window, with his back to* SYDNEY. SYDNEY, *settling on a page in "The Stuffed Owl."*) Listen to this. Here we have William Wordsworth on a bad day. (*Reading the lines as badly as they deserve to be read.*) "The piteous news so much it shocked her, She quite forgot to send the Doctor." (RICHARD *is silent.*) Are you all right? (*Slight pause.*) I think you are.

RICHARD. (*Turning.*) I don't know. I'm back in a house I knew, but the furniture's all been changed. I'll have to get used to it.

SYDNEY. You will. Just open one door at a time.

RICHARD. (*Facing him now.*) Sydney, I owe you something.

SYDNEY. (*Putting down the book and speaking quietly, but with emphasis.*) I want something.

RICHARD. (*Surprised, in spite of himself.*) What?

SYDNEY. Cathy.

RICHARD. (*Trying to get his bearings.*) Oh?

SYDNEY. Please let go of her.

RICHARD. (*Gathering the threads together.*) Sydney, I didn't know that you—I had no idea. I should have sensed—but I didn't.

SYDNEY. Never mind that. What do *you* feel about her?

RICHARD. (*Trying to be honest.*) There's no answer to that. I don't know. But I'd like to have the opportunity to find out.

SYDNEY. That's not enough. I want to marry her. I want to take care of her. She doesn't love me, but she may come to. And women have been known to settle for kindness.

RICHARD. And that would be *enough* for you?

SYDNEY. Yes.

RICHARD. You don't mean that.

SYDNEY. Oh, I've come to terms with myself. I know who I am—and what I look like. I know that hearts do not beat faster when I come into a room. People *become* fond of me.

RICHARD. You sound like you've taken a poll or something.

SYDNEY. I mean I *know.* I know that people have to be introduced to me four times before it takes. That's because I am so medium. Medium height, medium brown hair, medium blue eyes. . . . I should rob a bank. Nobody would be able to describe me. You should see me on the train! I don't trust the conductor, I ask *everybody* is this the train for Stamford. At a party, I'm the one that gets stuck all evening with the first person I meet.—Do you know—and I'm sure this is a clue to something—I never had a nickname. I guess I want a drink.

RICHARD. There's still some Scotch. Here, I'll fix it. (*Goes to make him one.*)

SYDNEY. Something else that's rather indicative. After a couple of hours in my company, women are apt to say "Sydney, you are really very sweet."

RICHARD. Something the matter with that?

SYDNEY. Yeah. I'll bet no one says it to you.

RICHARD. I'd have to think.

SYDNEY. Don't bother. I can tell you. They don't. What are you looking so shocked about?

RICHARD. Why did I suppose that you lived under a glass bell—that nothing ever touches you?

SYDNEY. Because I have gone to some pains to give that impression.

RICHARD. Why?

SYDNEY. It's a matter of the image, old boy. I've set myself up as a combination father-confessor and mother-hen, and now I'm rather stuck with it. And if I have moments of feeling less than Olympian, I just cover up for it. You know that all our offices have been moved down to the second floor. The official reason is because we need more space. The actual reason is that, once they put in those self-service elevators, I found that it gave me the cold shakes to go up as high as thirty. And I massage my head for five minutes every morning because somebody once told me it would keep my hair from falling out—and I lie awake nights yearning over a girl who probably will not have me in any case. (RICHARD *looks at him.*) Yes, Cathy. You understand that I love her exactly as if I were twenty-five and had a brand new contract from M-G-M.

RICHARD. I do understand.

SYDNEY. Then let her go. Hundreds of girls will fall in love with you. Let her be the one that got away.

RICHARD. (*Forcing a light vein.*) Hundreds? Surely you mean thousands? Are you trying to make me insecure? (SYDNEY *doesn't answer.*) Sydney, it's the end of the world for me, too, and I can make jokes. You can't?

SYDNEY. Apparently not.

RICHARD. What do you want me to tell you—that I won't see her again?

SYDNEY. No, I want you to see her.

RICHARD. Then what the hell have we been talking about?

SYDNEY. You realize she may go the rest of her life day-dreaming about you—and that won't do anybody any good. I want you to see her—see her and get rid of her. Finish it.

RICHARD. How do I do that?

SYDNEY. There are a number of ways, and you know all of them.

RICHARD. You want me to spit in her eye, or something.

SYDNEY. (*Quickly, with some passion.*) Don't you understand you'd be doing her a favor? Why should you breeze in and out of her life this way? Mid-century poet—loaded with charm—loaded with complexes! She'll be fifty years old and she'll still be having fantasies about you. The affair you don't get over is the one you never had. And don't look so puzzled. This is very simple. You have no plan to do anything about this girl. Or let me put it another way—you have no responsible plan. I do.

And all I'm asking you to do is to get the hell out of the manger.

CATHY. (*From off.*) Sydney? . . . Sydney?

(*They* BOTH *hear.*)

RICHARD. Are you going to answer?

SYDNEY. No, I'm leaving. It'll be as easy for you to do this now as any time. (*He goes to the door.*)

RICHARD. Sydney—I won't—you can't ask me—

SYDNEY. I do ask you. And I've never asked you for anything before.

RICHARD. No, that's impossible—she'd think I was a—

SYDNEY. That she won't have a high opinion of you isn't important. Maybe you ought to once do something that will give you a high opinion of yourself. I'll wait for her at the car.

(SYDNEY *goes.* RICHARD, *emotionally tangled, makes an abortive move toward the stairway, where* CATHY *is. Then he stops, his mind moving away from Cathy and back to what has most deeply involved him. He shakes his head slightly, as if to clear it, then focuses on the telephone. He goes to the desk, looks up a number in the telephone book, then dials it.*)

RICHARD. (*On phone.*) May I speak with Mrs. Baker, please? Richard Ford. (*Pause.*) Hello, Ginny, did I get you away from something? . . . Well, a couple of things. First, I'm sorry that I was so difficult— (*Making himself say it.*) —so rude—this afternoon. I know you're more or less accustomed to that from me, but—well, I'm sorry . . . The next thing is that I've changed my plans. I won't be going to California, so I'll be able to come to the ceremony at the hospital . . . No, I *wish* to come— unless you have some feeling that . . . Fine. Now what time is it, and how do I get there? . . . Sure, if you want to pick me up here, that'll be better still . . . Thank you.

. . . Tell the Howards I'll be happy to see *them* . . . Quarter to two, right. 'Bye. (*As* RICHARD *hangs up and turns from the phone, he sees that* CATHY *is now standing on the stairway.*) But soft! What light through yonder window breaks? It is my lady, and have you slept it off?

CATHY. I thought liquor was supposed to go to your head. It seems to have gone to my feet. I can't get my shoes back on. I guess my foot's asleep. When we were kids, we used to say that it felt like ginger-ale.

RICHARD. Sydney is outside in the car.

CATHY. Oh. (*She sits down.*)

RICHARD. This is something of a surprise. Do you pass out in the guest-room often?

CATHY. No, not often.

RICHARD. What I really want to know is what do people *do* about you? (*Reversing their first relationship, and kidding it.*) Shall I get you some black coffee? Aspirin? I'm told that at a time like this vanilla ice-cream is a help. You don't say anything.

CATHY. I figure I deserve the sarcasm, just as I deserve the hangover.

RICHARD. Oh! We've decided to be penitent!

CATHY. I haven't decided anything. I'm just trying to get my shoes on. (*She does get one on.*)

RICHARD. (*Settling near her.*) You know, you're getting off easy. Young ladies who lap it up in men's apartments frequently find that they have a great deal more to put back on than their shoes.

CATHY. (*Glancing at him.*) I didn't think you said things like that.

RICHARD. You didn't?

CATHY. (*Shaking her head.*) It's too easy. Too cheap.

RICHARD. I thought I was being realistic. Actually, I feel much cozier with you now that I discover you're not entirely the paragon you pretended to be. I feel the stirrings of new hope for you. Are you certain you want to put on that shoe? (*She looks puzzled.*) *I* think we'd be on the right track if we took the other one off. (*She looks alarmed; he grins.*) My dear, there are things in this world that are so much more fun than alcohol. (*Leans over to grasp her ankle.*) Come on, don't you think it's time you found out?

CATHY. (*Jumping up.*) Please—No.

RICHARD. Oh! You're going to play Saint Joan again!

CATHY. (*Lost.*) What do you mean?

RICHARD. I thought that *was* our relationship. You were Saint Joan and I was the Dauphin and you were going to make a man of me and put me back at the head of my armies.

CATHY. (*Trying to take it in.*) Was I really—as fatuous as that? I suppose I was. . . . I suppose I am. That's awful. (*Looking about her, hardly knowing for what.*) I'll have to watch that.

RICHARD. Please do. And let me tell you something about saintliness—a little of it goes a long way. It's like rice. It spreads. By the way, why did you think I left so abruptly a while ago?

CATHY. I didn't know.

RICHARD. But you must have had some thought—some little theory?

CATHY. Well, I—uh—

RICHARD. Yes, you—uh—

CATHY. (*Embarrassed but coming out with it.*) I guess I thought you didn't want to take advantage of me.

RICHARD. You know something? That's what I thought you thought. What a package we have here! This girl is pure—I mean, the driven snow cannot be mentioned in the same breath. But beyond that, mind you, above and beyond that she is catnip!

CATHY. I didn't say—

RICHARD. Such catnip that inflamed men are driven witless into the night! And now you are trying to make your big blue eyes look bigger. They are big enough. You know, luv, you *can* get too much of a good thing. Did it never occur to you that I left because you were the good thing I had quite enough of?

CATHY. (*Defensively, thrown but fighting.*) Sure, it

occurred to me! Everything occurred to me! And it's clear, clear, clear as can be that everything I said was silly and everything I did was wrong but why are you so harsh when I really was trying to help?

RICHARD. My dear, you are wasted on me. Had you thought of going to Africa and opening a little hospital?

(*NOTE: From this point in the play to the final curtain, either one of two alternate endings may be used, as the director prefers. They are both printed in the following pages, and if the second one is to be used, it should be picked up at this point.*)

(*He has turned away and is quietly arranging some papers on the desk.* CATHY *stares after him for a long moment, trying to understand. Then she does understand.*)

CATHY. Oh, Richard—you *are* trying to get rid of me! (*Her face lights up, incongruously.*) I think that's very nice of you.

RICHARD. (*Slowly turning toward her.*) *You* listened—!

CATHY. (*Dropping her eyes, and flustered.*) I know it was shabby of me. But in the beginning I was too wobbly—and then I was too embarrassed.

RICHARD. (*In half-exasperation.*) Then why did you let me go on?

CATHY. (*Honestly.*) It took me this long to figure out what you were doing. (*Trying to conceal tears.*) Isn't it silly? My feelings are just as hurt as if I didn't understand—

RICHARD. (*Grim.*) I hope you tell Sydney. I should get marks for this. (*Erratically.*) I'm glad you heard. (*With a sudden sigh, letting go of the energy the scene has required.*) Oh, God, I didn't have the stomach for this— or the energy. I'm thought to be a rather mercurial fellow —always leaping from mood to mood. But I'm not this mercurial. Not today.

CATHY. Oh, Richard— (*Catches herself.*) I was going

to say I *know*. But how could I know? I just think of what my grandfather used to say. The future holds no surprises. The surprises are all in the past. (*Trying to shake off what she has been feeling, speaking more lightly.*) You know, you look younger.

RICHARD. Younger than what?

CATHY. Than yesterday. All those little lines that sort of went down—sort of go up. (*Very slight pause.*) I suppose you'll go home now.

RICHARD. (*It's all new, and he must think it out.*) Yes, I'll *try* to go home. After the ceremony tomorrow, I'll get whatever plane I can, back to London. The house in Surrey—*our* house—has been closed for two years. I guess I'll have it opened up.

CATHY. (*Hardly knowing what to say.*) Well, it should be a relief to get back to the house in Surrey—

RICHARD. A relief? (*Considers it.*) I don't know. What has happened to me is that I have been given permission to remember. I'll have to see if I can stand it.

CATHY. (*On an impulse.*) Richard, I knew all along that there was nothing wrong between you and your wife.

RICHARD. (*Looking at her, frowning.*) How did you know?

CATHY. (*A bit more hesitant now, but seeing it through.*) Because . . . when you talked about her, I felt—jealous.

RICHARD. (*Firmly.*) Cathy, you know that it would be right, absolutely right, for you to marry Sydney.

CATHY. (*Looking up.*) Because he's so nice?

RICHARD. That, too. But more than that. You're looking for a universe that's small enough to order around. Sydney would provide that for you.

CATHY. Is that what I'm looking for?

RICHARD. And as you said yesterday—the important thing in a relationship is the reason.

CATHY. (*A sudden flare.*) Don't tell me what I said yesterday. (*Pulling herself back.*) That was a whole year ago. I'm somebody else now.

RICHARD. (*Gently, and with a smile.*) Well, whoever you are—you're still seven years old.

CATHY. (*With a grin.*) Oh, I'm coming along. Do you realize that in the space of twenty-four hours I kissed a practically strange man and got drunk and it's probably good for my character?

RICHARD. But could that be?

CATHY. (*More seriously.*) Maybe I won't be so intolerant. I used to say, "Why do people *do* these things?" Now I know why. Because—at the time—they *wanted* to. That's something to know. The thing is, I was giving myself credit for having high standards when, to tell the truth, I was just uninterested. (*She is suddenly self-conscious.*) But now it seems clear to me that because my mother married for love five times is no reason why I can't marry for love once.

RICHARD. Cathy—

CATHY. (*With a start.*) Oh, Lord! You think I mean *you.*

RICHARD. Don't you?

CATHY. Oh, no. Oh, dearest Richard, no. I'm not confused about the situation. You reached out for me once—when you were desperate. You're no longer desperate. And when you reach out again, it will be for somebody quite different.

RICHARD. Like who?

CATHY. I'll read about her. (*She has got the other shoe on.*)

RICHARD. You going? Right *now?*

CATHY. (*Getting up.*) I can't keep Sydney waiting forever.

RICHARD. Ah, but you *do* keep Sydney waiting forever.

CATHY. (*Extending her hand.*) Goodbye, Richard.

RICHARD. Will I see you again? (*He notices her expression.*) What's that wan little smile about?

CATHY. Because *you* said it. I promised myself that no matter what other stupid thing I said, I wouldn't ask you that.

RICHARD. Why not?

CATHY. Because I *won't* see you again. (*This isn't a refusal, just a premonition. There is a pause, and she explains.*) It doesn't feel that way. It feels so *over*.

RICHARD. How can it be over when it never really started? (*Simply, definitely.*) Cathy, I'll be back in May and I will call you.

CATHY. I may not even place the name. I'll say *who?* —Richard who?

RICHARD. (*Going right on.*) We'll do something marvelous and idiotic. We'll take a bus tour of Chinatown. Or ride on a ferry. Have you ever been on the Staten Island Ferry?

CATHY. (*Ruefully.*) I live on Staten Island.

(*They* BOTH *laugh.*)

RICHARD. Well, then, we'll just walk around the Village and talk.

CATHY. (*With no real conviction.*) Okay.

RICHARD. Don't you believe it?

CATHY. Do you believe it?

RICHARD. I have to.

CATHY. Have to?

RICHARD. The alternative is that I *never* see you again. Now, I had a chance to consider that possibility, and it didn't *seem* possible. (*Wryly.*) When I was getting rid of you— (*Straighter.*) you looked so bewildered, like a little girl who got lost at the circus. And I thought —this is wrong, this is *wrong*. (*Between his teeth.* CATHY *puts her fingers to his lips to stop the expletive. He obliges her by re-forming the sentence.*) I mean, I found it more painful that I would have supposed.

CATHY. I'm glad. (*Very slight pause.*) Goodbye, Richard. (*She leans up and kisses him on the cheek, then goes to the door.*)

RICHARD. (*As she looks back from the door, speaking with thoughtful precision.*) I found it a *lot* more painful than I would have supposed.

CATHY. (*Smiling.*) Poor Richard. And he's so talented.

(*She is going, as:*)

## THE CURTAIN FALLS

(*NOTE: Alternate ending follows, to be picked up from Page 74.*)

CATHY. (*Her voice softens in surprise and discovery.*) Oh, you must love me a lot!

RICHARD. What?

CATHY. You're trying to send me away for my own good. Well, being mean isn't the way to do it. That just gets my hair up.

RICHARD. But Cathy darling—I must send you away. Please let me.

CATHY. Why?

RICHARD. Do you know it would be right for you to marry Sydney?

CATHY. Because he's so nice?

RICHARD. That, too, but more. You're looking for a universe that is small enough to order around and Sydney would provide that for you.

CATHY. That was yesterday. That was a whole year ago. I'm somebody new now.

RICHARD. But Cathy, I'm patched goods. I'm not fit for you and you don't want me.

CATHY. But I do.

RICHARD. But you don't know me.

CATHY. (*Rises to* RICHARD.) All I know is that because my mother married for love five times is no reason why I can't marry for love once.

RICHARD. You think you're ready for me now?

CATHY. No, I think you're ready for me. Something has changed. All those little lines that sort of went down, sort of go up. What happened?

RICHARD. (*Crosses* R.) I discovered something. I dis-

covered that love can come in the side door. The one
you didn't know was left open.

CATHY. I knew all along you loved Angela.

RICHARD. Why?

CATHY. Because when you talked about her I felt
jealous.

RICHARD. (*Crosses above table.*) I'll tell you a few
things you don't know. I'm a wilderness of bad habits. I
burn cigarette holes in all the blankets. I leave beer cans
in the bathroom.

CATHY. I'll get them out of there.

RICHARD. I leave my overcoats behind me in taxicabs.
I get up in the middle of the night and make egg sandwiches.

CATHY. I'll fry the eggs.

RICHARD. (*Crosses L. upstairs.*) And I'm impossible
to live with.

CATHY. (*Crosses to foot of stairs.*) So was Picasso
and the people that loved him just nearly went crazy,
but they wouldn't have had it any different.

RICHARD. You mustn't have illusions about me. I'm
a second-rate poet.

CATHY. You'll improve.

RICHARD. (*Coming down.*) All right. I'll tell you the
truth. I'm marvelous.

CATHY. No you're not. You're distrustful. You don't
believe in the possibility of Richard, and you're going to
have doubts all over again next Thursday. And some of
them will be about me and I don't care. I used to be in
love with a poet, and now I'm in love with you.

RICHARD. Cathy, the way you operate is extraordinary.
You really are like a bumblebee.

CATHY. How do you mean?

RICHARD. Scientists have proved that the wings of
the bumblebee are far too small to carry the weight of
its body. But the bumblebee, not knowing this, flies
anyway.

CATHY. I'll change.

RICHARD. Don't you dare! You know I've never met anyone so wonderfully all one color. (*She kisses him.*) We'll go out and celebrate.

CATHY. Let's do something idiotic.

RICHARD. (*Crosses U.R. for Cathy's coat.*) We'll take a tour of Chinatown. We'll take a ride on the Staten Island Ferry. Have you ever been on the Staten Island Ferry?

CATHY. I live on Staten Island.

RICHARD. Then let's sit here and have a picnic.

CATHY. There's nothing in the icebox.

RICHARD. (*Gets his cap and coat.*) We'll go to a supermarket. Let's buy sausages and fancy cakes.

CATHY. And if we see your little girl on the steps—

RICHARD. Mary Rose Cavanaugh.

CATHY. We'll invite her to tea.

RICHARD. Yes, she must be the first to know.

CATHY. We'll get a shopping basket and dump things into it.

RICHARD. Wait a minute. What do we need with a shopping basket? (*He gets her enormous bag from under the desk and throws it over his shoulder.*) Come on. . . .

(*They exit as:*)

*THE CURTAIN FALLS*

# PROPERTY PLOT

## *ACT ONE*

CHECK: No snow

DOORS: Front open. Bath and bedroom closed

D. L.: Desk with swivel chair.

*On desk:*
  Glass with cigarette butt in it
  2 empty beer cans
  Cigarettes and matches
  Richard's sweater

*In drawer:*
  Passport folder
Waste basket D. S. of desk
Suitcase under stairs:
  8 shirts, 3 shorts, 6 pairs of socks, 2 T-shirts, carton of players, ties
Richard's shoes under stairs
Richard's tie on chair by bathroom door
U. S. of bathroom door shelf with picture frame and wrought iron candlestick with candle
S. R. of window cabinet with 2 decanters and lamp

*Kitchen:*
  Door on marks
  U. S. refrigerator
    Carton of milk inside
  Sink D. S. of refrigerator
    Glass U. S. edge
  Stove D. S. of sink
  Prop table:
    Tray: 2 mugs, 3 spoons, 2 napkins, coffee pot and sugar bowl
    3 glasses
    Bottle of scotch
    2 plates with napkins
    1 mug

*On platform:*
  Chair D. S. L.
    Bottle D. S.
    2 glasses D. S. with remains of drinks
    Ashtray wih butts D. S.
  Hassock on Act One marks
  Stove U. S. L. (cloth over grate)—
    S. R. box of fireplace matches
    S. R. bottle of vodka with vodka
  Sofa:
    Telephone D. S. R. (Jack unplugged by platform outlet)
    4 books on floor U. S. L. end
  Coffee table in front of sofa:
    Ashtray with butts
    Silver cigarette box with cigarettes
    2 glasses with remains of drinks
    1 bottle
  In front of coffee table:
    Upright liquor carton with 7 bottles
    1 bottle in front of carton
  2 bottles in front of platform by phone jack (1 with scotch)

*Bedroom:*
  Richard's coat and hat
  2 empty beer cans

*Bathroom:*
  Shaving kit
  Shaving brush
  Shaving cream
  Hair oil
  Comb
  Brush
  Toothpaste
  Toothbrush
  Richard's bathrobe

*Off Right:*
  Purse (Cathy):
    Clipboard, with pencil attached
    6 unsharpened pencils in rubber band with pencil sharpener
      attached
    Kleenex
    Postcard with writing
    Pad

Papers (Sydney) :
  List of appointments
  Letters (NBC, CBS)
Money (Sydney)
Bag with sandwiches (Cathy)
Typewriter (Cathy)
Note pad (McFarland)
Manila envelope (McFarland)
Stuffed Owl (book) (McFarland)
LOOK Magazine (SYDNEY)
Angela's journal in manila envelope (Ginny)

## ACT TWO

*Strike:*
  Tray with sandwiches, mugs, from coffee table
  Typewriter from desk to coffee table
  Cloth with butts from fireplace
  Mug from desk

*On Coffee Table:*
  Electric coffee pot plugged in
  Mug and spoon
  Trans World Airline tickets
  Sugar bowl
  Typewriter with letter in it
Large plain cushion S. R. of coffee table on floor
Bottle of scotch on floor U. S. of coffee table
Hassock on Act Two marks
Richard's cap and coat on coat rack

Desk :
  Telephone plugged in jack
  Envelope
Richard's sweater on sofa

U. S. Cabinet :
  2 glasses and bottle of scotch

*Off Right:*
  Cathy's shoes in purse
  Letters to answer on clipboard and in purse

*Check Snow:*
  Windows, fence, ground cloth, and tree with snow
  All doors closed

*ACT THREE*

Typewriter in case on desk
Plain pillow on edge of platform
Shoes from purse D. R. area by large cushions

U. S. cabinet: 2 glasses
Coffee table: bottle of scotch
Cathy's boots U. S. on floor
Cathy's coat on desk chair
Cathy's bag under desk—everything in it
Richard's slippers under sofa U. L.

D. L. corner of platform: Cointreau bottle and glass
Hassock against S. L. side of coffee table
Bathroom and bedroom door closed

# COSTUME PLOT

## *ACT ONE*

CATHY:
Brown, tan, blue checked dress with tan leather belt
Tan flat shoes
Tan gloves
Tan polo coat with 8 buttons
Extra large brown purse
Olive figured stockings
Gold wrist watch

RICHARD:
Dark brown slacks
White shirt
Brown bedroom slippers
Large bulky white sweater
Green knit tie
Brown suede shoes with crepe soles
Khaki trench coat
Checked cap
Black socks

SYDNEY:
Gray flannel suit
Blue striped button-down shirt
Maroon tie
Black shoes
Black socks
Black and white tweed top coat

McFARLAND:
Tan tweed sport coat
Green and white checked button-down shirt
Black and yellow striped bow tie
Gray slacks
Maroon socks
Brown loafers

## *ACT TWO*

CATHY:
Tan suede jumper dress
Tan crew neck sweater
Knee length tan boots
Tan figured stockings

*Repeat Act One:*
    Shoes
    Coat
    Purse
    Gloves

RICHARD:
  Green plaid sport shirt

  *Repeat Act One:*
    Slacks
    Coat
    Sweater
    Shoes
    Socks

SYDNEY:
  Blue pin-stripe suit
  Dark blue and black striped tie

  *Repeat Act One:*
    Shoes
    Socks
    Coat
    Shirt

GINNY:
  Brown sleeveless dress with gold pin
  Dark brown suede low-heeled shoes
  Dark brown suede purse with chain handles
  Brown gloves
  Ranch mink coat

## *ACT THREE*

CATHY:
  *Repeat Act Two*

RICHARD:
  *Repeat Act Two*

SYDNEY:
  *Repeat Act Two*

McFARLAND:
  *Repeat Act Two*

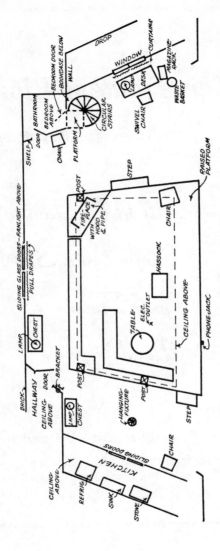

SCENE DESIGN

"POOR RICHARD"

# *The Tandem Library*

*A Selection of 20 Plays from*

*All in the Family*

*Sanford and Son*

*Good Times*

*Maude*

For details of titles available and royalty fees apply to Samuel French, Inc.

# The Happy Hunter

## (ALL GROUPS)
## Comedy—CHARLES FEYDEAU

### English Adaptation by Barnett Shaw
#### 7 Men, 3 Women—2 Interiors

Chandel tells Yvonne he is going hunting with Castillo, but when Castillo turns up unexpectedly, she sees the hoax, and therefore decides to yield to Roussel's amorous advances, going to his bachelor den with him. But, across the hall, Chandel is having a rendezvous with Madame Castillo. A hectic evening ensues, complicated by an eccentric landlady and by the appearance of Yvonne's nephew, whose girl friend used to live there. The police, seeking Madame Castillo's lover, grab Roussel, while Chandel escapes through the window and runs off with Roussel's trousers. The mix-up unravels in act three, with one surprise after the other, Yvonne winning all tricks while her husband gets the punishment.

**ROYALTY, $35-$25**

# A Gown for His Mistress

## (Little Theatre) Farce
## GEORGE FEYDEAU

### English Translation by Barnett Shaw
#### 4 Men, 6 Females—Interior
#### Can be played 1900 Period or Chic Modern

**A wild and saucy matrimonial mix-up by the celebrated author of A FLEA IN HER EAR.**

Dr. Moulineaux stays out all night after a futile attempt to meet his mistress, Suzanne, at the Opera Ball. He tells his wife he has been up all night with a friend, Bassinet, who is near death, but at that moment Bassinet walks in. Upbraided by his mother-in-law for his infidelity, he decides he must no longer allow Suzanne to pretend to be a patient. For a hide-away, he rents an apartment that formerly belonged to a dressmaker. In Act II he is courting Suzanne in his new apartment when her husband walks in. Posing as a dressmaker he gets rid of the husband momentarily, but is caught in a desperate entanglement when his wife, his mother-in-law, Bassinet, and Bassinet's wife appear. In Act III, Moulineaux's household is in an uproar but he manages to lie his way out of it all with the help of Bassinet who has a photograph that seems to solve everything. Outstanding male and female roles. The play moves rapidly and is an excellent work-out for alert actors and actresses.

**ROYALTY, $35-$25**

**#12**

# HANDBOOK

## for

### THEATRICAL APPRENTICES
### By Dorothy Lee Tompkins

Here is a common sense book on theatre, fittingly sub-titled, "A Practical Guide in All Phases of Theatre." Miss Tompkins has wisely left art to the artists and written a book which deals only with the practical side of the theatre. All the jobs of the theatre are categorized, from the star to the person who sells soft drinks at intermission. Each job is defined, and its basic responsibilities given in detail. An invaluable manual for every theatre group in explaining to novices the duties of apprenticeship, and in reassessing its own organizational structure and functions.

"If you are an apprentice or are just aspiring in any capacity, then you'll want to read and own Dorothy Lee Tompkins' A HANDBOOK FOR THEATRICAL APPRENTICES. It should be required reading for any drama student anywhere and is a natural for the amateur in any phase of the theatre."—George Freedley, Morning Telegraph.

"It would be helpful if the HANDBOOK FOR THE-ATRICAL APPRENTICES were in school or theatrical library to be used during each production as a guide to all participants."—Florence E. Hill, Dramatics Magazine.

# *Witness for the Prosecution*

## Melodrama—3 Acts

### By AGATHA CHRISTIE

#### 17 Men, 5 Women. Interior—Modern Costumes

*Winner of New York Critics Circle Award and the Antoinette Perry Award. One of the greatest mystery melodramas in years.*

The story is that of a likable young drifter who is suspected of bashing in the head of a middle-aged, wealthy spinster who has willed her tidy estate to him. His only alibi is the word of his wife, a queer customer, indeed, who, in the dock, repudiates the alibi and charges him with the murder. Then a mystery woman appears with damaging letters against the wife and the young man is freed. We learn, however, that the mystery woman is actually the wife, who has perjured herself because she felt direct testimony for her husband woud not have freed him. But when the young man turns his back on his wife for another woman, we realize he really was the murderer. Then Miss Christie gives us a triple-flip ending that leaves the audience gasping, while serving up justice to the young man.

#### (ROYALTY, $50-$25.)

# 𝕿𝖍𝖊 𝕸𝖔𝖚𝖘𝖊𝖙𝖗𝖆𝖕

*The longest-run straight play in London history.*

## Melodrama—3 Acts

### By AGATHA CHRISTIE

#### 5 Men, 3 Women—Interior

*The author of Ten Little Indians and Witness for the Prosecution comes forth with another English hit.*

About a group of strangers stranded in a boarding house during a snow storm, one of whom is a murderer. The suspects include the newly married couple who run the house, a spinster, an architect, a retired Army major, a strange little man who claims his car overturned in a drift, and a feminine jurist. Into their midst comes a policeman, traveling on skiis. He no sooner arrives than the jurist is killed. To get to the rationale of the murderer's pattern, the policeman probes the background of everyone present, and rattles a lot of skeletons. Another famous Agatha Christie switch finish! Chalk up another superb intrigue for the foremost mystery writer of her half century. Posters and publicity.

#### (ROYALTY, $50-$25.)

# *Going Ape*

## NICK HALL

### (Little Theatre.) Farce.
### 3 male, 2 female—Interior

This hilarious and almost indescribable farce has some serious undertones. Rupert, an idealistic and romantic young orphan, has come to his uncle's house to commit suicide. This proves to be no easy matter. For one thing he is constantly attended by his uncle's attractive nurse/secretary. He is also constantly interrupted by a stream of visitors, at first fairly normal, but increasingly incredible. Rupert realizes that all the visitors are the same three people, and his attention is drawn toward understanding the preposterously Victorian plot in which he is trapped, and which, in a startlingly theatrical climax, he begins to understand. "An intricate plot with subtle foreshadowing and a grab bag of surprises . . . some of the funniest characters you'll ever see molded into a tight dramatic package."— News, Fort Myers. "Every scene transcends not only the imagination, but melds into a literally death-defying whole. It's fast, like 2,000 mph . . . a play as old and as contemporary as today." Sarasota Journal. "Going Ape is truly zany . . . the wackiness is infectious." —Time.

### (Royalty, $50-$25.)

# *Eat Your Heart Out*

## NICK HALL

### (Little Theatre.) Comedy.
### 3 male, 2 female—Interior

In this theatrical comedy Charlie, an out of work actor currently employed as a waiter, takes the audience through a sequence of hilarious encounters in a succession of Manhattan restaurants. By changing the tablecloths during the course of the action the basic setting of three tables and six chairs becomes a variety of New York restaurants, both elegant and shabby. The scenes change, the action is uninterrupted and the comedy never stops. The other performers play several parts: the girl desperately trying to eat snails and oysters to please her fiance; the middle-aged couple whose marriage is breaking up; the lovers so intent on each other they cannot order dinner; the rich, embittered astrologer; the timid man who never gets a waiter; the agents, directors, actors, and waiters. An amusing gallery of characters whose stories intertwine and finally involve Charlie. The author of "Accommodations" has written a very funny, contemporary play that is also a serious comedy of backstage life. ". . . a sharp, stunning play. It'll make you howl—but better yet, it might even make you sniffle a bit."—Fort Lauderdale News. "Tightly written and very, very entertaining. I recommend it enthusiastically."—Miami Herald. ". . . About as good as anything I've ever seen in dinner theater . . ."—Fort Lauderdale Times.

### (Royalty, $50-$25.)

# The Gingerbread Lady

## NEIL SIMON
### (Little Theatre) Comedy-Drama
### 3 Men, 3 Women—Interior

Maureen Stapleton played the Broadway part of a popular singer who has gone to pot with booze and sex. We meet her at the end of a ten-week drying out period at a sanitarium, when her friend, her daughter, and an actor try to help her adjust to sobriety. But all three have the opposite effect on her. The friend is so constantly vain she loses her husband; the actor, a homosexual, is also doomed, and indeed loses his part three days before an opening; and the daughter needs more affection than she can spare her mother. Enter also a former lover louse, who ends up giving her a black eye. The birthday party washes out, the gingerbread lady falls off the wagon and careens onward to her own tragic end.

"He has combined an amusing comedy with the atmosphere of great sadness. His characteristic wit and humor are at their brilliant best, and his serious story of lost misfits can often be genuinely and deeply touching."—N.Y. Post. "Contains some of the brightest dialogue Simon has yet composed."—N.Y. Daily News. "Mr. Simon's play is as funny as ever—the customary avalanche of hilarity, and landslide of pure unbuttoned joy . . . Mr. Simon is a funny, funny man—with tears running down his cheek."—N.Y. Times.

### Royalty $50-$35

# The Sunshine Boys

## NEIL SIMON
### (All Groups) Comedy
### 5 Men, 2 Women

An ex-vaudeville team, Al Lewis and Willie Clarke, in spite of playing together for forty-three years, have a natural antipathy for one another. (Willie resents Al's habit of poking a finger in his chest, or perhaps accidentally spitting in his face). It has been eleven years since they have performed together, when along comes CBS-TV, who is preparing a "History of Comedy" special, that will of course include Willie and Al—the "Lewis and Clark" team back together again. In the meantime, Willie has been doing spot commercials, like for Schick (the razor blade shakes) or for Frito-Lay potato chips (he forgets the name), while Al is happily retired. The team gets back together again, only to have Al poke his finger in Willie's chest, and accidentally spit in his face.

". . . the most delightful play Mr. Simon has written for several seasons and proves why he is the ablest current author of stage humor."—Watts, N. Y. Post. "None of Simon's comedies has been more intimately written out of love and a bone-deep affinity with the theatrical scene and temperament." Time. ". . . another hit for Neil Simon in this shrewdly balanced, splendidly performed and rather touching slice of the show-biz life."—Watt, New York Daily News. "(Simon) . . . writes the most dependably crisp and funny dialogue around . . . always well-set and polished to a high lustre."—WABC-TV. ". . . a vaudeville act within a vaudeville act . . . Simon has done it again."—WCBS-TV.

### Royalty $50-$35

# THE LADY WHO CRIED FOX!!!
## (LITTLE THEATRE—COMEDY)
### By EDWARD CLINTON

#### 3 men, 2 women—Interior

When a jealous actor who's always on the road, finds out his wife has taken on a young male roommate to meet expenses, the show does not go on. He immediately returns home to find out what's going on. The roommate, an inventor who likes to roller skate, is caught in the middle between a jealous husband and frustrated wife. Eventually, all five of the characters get into the act and the result is just plain fun. ". . . punch and humor . . . a funny play. . . ." —Miami Herald. ". . . clever script . . . intriguing sense of humor coupled with a powerful knack for drama. . . ." —Fort Lauderdale News. ". . . funny, delightful and above all devoid of the off color material so many writers feel is essential. . . ." —Hollywood, Fla. Sun Tattler.

**(Royalty, $50-$35.)**

---

# NOT WITH MY DAUGHTER
## (LITTLE THEATRE—COMEDY)
### By JAY CHRISTOPHER

#### 3 men, 3 women—Interior

Will Gray suddenly has a problem. His 18-year-old daughter appears at his "swinging singles" apartment door. It seems Will and his neighbor, Rip Tracy, a velvet-voiced radio Dee Jay have a penchant for juggling girls like antacid tablets. Poor Will has a go-go girl in the living room—with her motor running—and a devoted young lady in the bedroom—but that's o.k. since she loves him. Rip has a girl in his apartment already when Will calls on him to also entertain the go-go girl. Then Will's daughter appears to complicate matters further—not only are explanations in order—but daughter has problems of her own. How it all is resolved will leave the audience limp with laughter. An adult play with not one leering joke. It's all in fun. "Funny? Absolutely." —High Point, N.C. Enterprise. ". . . a laugh riot . . ." —Greensboro, N.C. Daily News. ". . . fast-paced farce with as many laughs as you can handle in one sitting." —Lexington, Ky. Herald.

**(Royalty, $50-$25.)**

# MELODRAMAS

## GAY NINETY TYPE

**CAUGHT IN THE VILLAIN'S WEB;**
  or More Sinned Against Than Sinning

**CURSE OF AN ACHING HEART;**
  or Trapped in the Spider's Web

**DEADWOOD DICK;** or A Game of Gold

**DIRTY WORK AT THE CROSSROADS;**
  or Tempted, Tried and True

**DRUNKARD, The;** or The Fallen Saved

**EAST LYNNE**

**FATE WORSE THAN DEATH;**
  or Adrift in Life's Sea

**FIREMAN'S FLAME**—Musical

**FOR HER CHEILD'S SAKE;**
  or Her First False Step

**LILY, THE FELON'S DAUGHTER**

**NO MOTHER TO GUIDE HER;**
  or More To Be Pitied Than Censured

**ON THE BRIDGE AT MIDNIGHT**

**PURE AS THE DRIVEN SNOW,**
  or A Working Girl's Secret

**STREETS OF NEW YORK**

**STREETS OF NEW YORK**—Musical

**TEN NIGHTS IN A BARROOM**

**TEN NIGHTS IN A BARROOM**—Musical

**UNCLE TOM'S CABIN**

**WEST OF EAST LYNNE**

## SAMUEL FRENCH, Inc.

25 West 45th St.          7623 Sunset Blvd.
NEW YORK 10036          HOLLYWOOD 90046

#44

# DON'T DRINK THE WATER

## By WOODY ALLEN

### FARCE

#### 12 men, 4 women—Interior

A CASCADE OF COMEDY FROM ONE OF OUR FUNNIEST CO-MEDIANS, and a solid hit on Broadway, this affair takes place inside an American embassy behind the Iron Curtain. An American tourist, caterer by trade, and his family of wife and daughter rush into the embassy two steps ahead of the police, who suspect them of spying and picture-taking. But it's not much of a refuge, for the ambassador is absent and his son, now in charge, has been expelled from a dozen countries and the whole continent of Africa. Nevertheless, they carefully and frantically plot their escape, and the ambassador's son and the caterer's daughter even have time to fall in love. "Because Mr. Allen is a working comedian himself, a number of the lines are perfectly agreeable . . . and there's quite a delectable bit of business laid out by the author and manically elaborated by the actor. . . . The gag is pleasantly outrageous and impeccably performed."—*N. Y. Times.* "Moved the audience to great laughter. . . . Allen's imagination is daffy, his sense of the ridiculous is keen and gags snap, crackle and pop."—*N. Y. Daily News.* "It's filled with funny lines. . . . A master of bright and hilarious dialogue."—*N. Y. Post.*

(Slightly restricted. Royalty, $50-$25, where available.)


# THE ODD COUPLE

## By NEIL SIMON

### COMEDY

#### 6 men, 2 women—Interior

NEIL SIMON'S THIRD SUCCESS in a row begins with a group of the boys assembled for cards in the apartment of a divorced fellow, and if the mess of the place is any indication, it's no wonder that his wife left him. Late to arrive is another fellow who, they learn, has just been separated from his wife. Since he is very meticulous and tense, they fear he might commit suicide, and so go about locking all the windows. When he arrives, he is scarcely allowed to go to the bathroom alone. As life would have it, the slob bachelor and the meticulous fellow decide to bunk together—with hilarious results. The patterns of their own disastrous marriages begin to reappear in this arrangement; and so this too must end. "The richest comedy Simon has written and purest gold for any theatregoer. . . . This glorious play."—*N. Y. World-Telegram & Sun.* "His skill is not only great but constantly growing. . . . There is scarcely a moment that is not hilarious."—*N. Y. Times.*

(Royalty, $50-$35.)